The Great Revolutions

THE CHINESE REVOLUTION

The Great Revolutions

Tibor Mende

THE CHINESE REVOLUTION

 Thames and Hudson

© THAMES AND HUDSON LONDON 1961
PRINTED IN GREAT BRITAIN BY
EBENEZER BAYLIS AND SON LTD WORCESTER

Contents

Foreword

GREAT TURNING POINTS OF HISTORY rarely have definite dates of origin. The Chinese Revolution is no exception.
To try and fix its beginning in time is an arbitrary act of
selection.

The obvious choice would be 1911. It was the year when the
Empire fell and the Republic was born. Yet by then China had
been in ferment for some time. So, one ought to go farther
back in time. And the date perhaps best suited to mark the
beginning of the story might be 1895. It was in that year that,
after a brief war, China was defeated by Japan.

The ring of despoilers was closing in on China. But the
Empire was still intact and apparently prosperous. Its self-
confidence was not yet shaken too much and, at least superficially, the old imperial edifice appeared to resist change. Yet
all of a sudden Japan's triumph ruined the picture the Chinese
Empire had of itself. The victor was a neighbour who had
been considered weak and inferior. Unlike the other powers
which had humiliated China, Japan was fellow-Asian. In fact,
it was the first Asian country which had consciously adapted
the West's technology.

The shock was as great as it was unexpected. China had to
realize that she was powerless either to modernize herself or to
resist. And clearly, the price of continued immobility was the
threat of actual dismemberment. From that moment onward
no self-deception could any longer conceal the fact that the
country had fallen far behind in the world-wide race for power
and material betterment or that, left unremedied, its situation
would further and rapidly deteriorate. The need for change
became obvious. And with the consequent search for new ideas
and methods China entered a pre-revolutionary phase that was
to last over fifteen years.

In a sense it was like the prologue introducing a Greek play.
It defined the antagonists and the passions which were to

U . S . S .

SIN

Tarim R.

TIBET

Lhas

China today

Relief, provinces,
principal towns

INDIA

under 1500 ft.

1500–8000 ft.

over 8000 ft.

BU

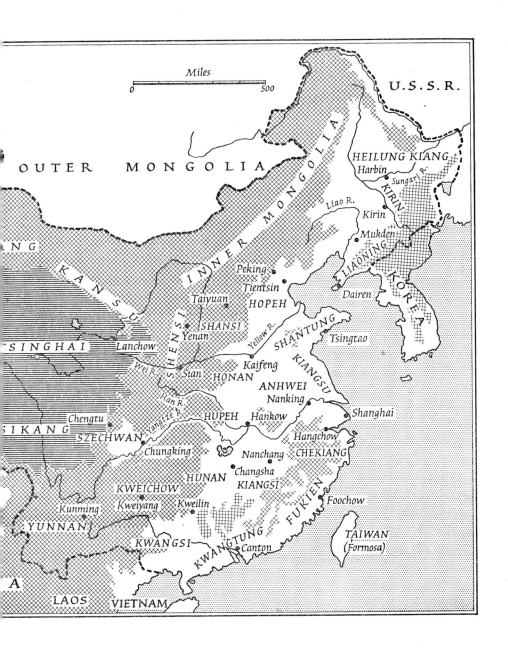

dominate the stage. Then, in 1911, the curtain went up on the first act of the drama. It was by far the longest of the three to come. The Empire collapsed and the Republic was proclaimed. It revealed a confused and prostrate China wooed by two seducers: the Kuomintang and the Communists. When the lights went up again in 1927, the two were in mortal battle and during the ten years of that second act the Kuomintang appeared to be victorious. But in 1937 the third act began with the war against the Japanese invader. And during the next twelve years the stage was lively with changes, ending, in 1949, in the Communists' triumph.

Within those fifty-four years a quarter of mankind changed its institutions, its way of life and its collective aspirations. The story of that crowded half-century is also the history of the Chinese Revolution. To discern its main strands and—however simplified—to describe its unfolding, is the aim of this book.

Part One

The Twilight of the Empire

ON 17 APRIL 1895, A TREATY, signed in the Japanese city of Shimonoseki, put an end to the first war between China and Japan. By far the larger of the two countries had been swiftly and decisively defeated. The victor's terms were harsh. China had to cede Formosa and the Pescadores, Port Arthur as well as the Liaotung Peninsula in Manchuria. China also agreed to pay a heavy indemnity and, even worse, she was forced to accept the independence of Korea, a country she had considered her vassal since the fifteenth century.

Both China and Japan had been manipulating political factions in Korea. The first, to maintain her rights and the second, in order to gain a foothold in a neighbouring country which was henceforth to serve both her economic and strategic ambitions. When it had come to a show-down, China had been defeated with unexpected speed. Hostilities lasted but nine months. The Chinese fleet surrendered. It had been paralysed by lack of ammunition and its battleships had to be used as transports. Nor were China's land forces more effective. They had been divided up among local governors and they lacked the will to fight. Their equipment had been archaic and the money destined for the purchase of modern arms had evidently gone to line the pockets of corrupt officials.

In contrast, Japan's troops were well equipped, disciplined and were led by competent officers. They had crossed the Yalu River without great difficulty and spread out into Manchuria. The Chinese colossus proved to be unable to fight while Japan, relying on her modern techniques, appeared irresistible.

The shock was great and the consequences manifold. Foreign interference in China, steadily gaining momentum since the Opium War, was entering upon a new phase. Encouraged by her spectacular success, Japan now began to insist that she should share all the privileges, including extra-territoriality, which the European powers had secured for themselves. As for

13

the western powers, spurred on both by the latest demonstration of China's helplessness and by their fear that Japan might claim an undue share of the spoils, they began to step up their own preparations to carve up the country into spheres of influence.

It was under the impact of these developments that Chinese complacency and the myth of superiority were beginning to yield to nation-wide soul-searching. Within five years there occurred a popular revolt against foreign encroachment. In another eleven years the monarchy itself was swept away with all the age-old institutions it had stood for.

Deceptive stability

On the eve of the Sino-Japanese war China had presented a misleading picture. Since the end of the Taiping rebellion in 1864 peace reigned all over the country and, after the failure of the rising in Sinkiang, even in the border areas. The treaty ports were flourishing. China had no external debts to pay. The last generation of mandarins was administering the country with tolerable efficiency. The finances of the State appeared to be sound and, internally at least, the prestige of the dynasty and of the Empire stood high.

Yet all this was deceptive like the venerable grandeur of a tree the inside of which termites have already eaten away. The internal economy of the country had been moving towards a dangerous disequilibrium. There were no spectacular complications with foreign powers but the authority and the liberty of action of the Chinese Government were gradually undermined. If administrative routine avoided a breakdown it was not flexible enough to prepare for change and adaptation. While the absence of major upheavals helped the rapid expansion of population, progress was too slow to bring about material improvement. Moreover, the Taiping rebellion bequeathed to China the semi-modern army. If it was strong enough to tyrannize the population or to further the ambitions of the men who commanded the various factions, it was inadequate to defend the country against foreign aggression.

Thus, as the century progressed, more and more treaties had been forced on China, each strengthening the economic and political fetters destined to prepare her for a semi-colonial era. It was at that moment that the Sino-Japanese war opened a new chapter in China's relations with the rest of the world.

The western powers had no illusions about the significance of Japan's victory. A new power, geographically far better placed than any western country, was claiming its place in the ring. This set off a chain-reaction of claims and counter-claims for economic and strategic advantages. The picking of privileges, proceeding at a leisurely pace since the Opium War, was turning into a race. Within a few years China was threatened with actual partition.

About a week after the signature of the Treaty of Shimonoseki, Russia, France and Germany presented a joint demand that Japan should return the Liaotung Peninsula to China. Reluctantly, Japan had to yield. But the bill for this 'service' was soon presented.

Between 1897 and 1899 Russia herself obtained a lease of the Liaotung Peninsula in South Manchuria, including the ports of Dairen and Port Arthur, as well as various mining and railroad concessions. France secured comparable privileges in 1895 in South-west China. Seizing the occasion of the murder of two German missionaries in 1897, within a year Germany secured a ninety-nine-year leasehold in Shantung province, completed by various other economic privileges. In the meantime, Great Britain expanded her commercial foothold, gained contracts for railway building, secured a lease of the northern port of Weihaiwai, and also took a ninety-nine-year lease on part of the mainland opposite the island of Hong Kong. Like sharks biting off chunks of an inert body, Great Britain, France, Germany, Russia, Japan, Italy and Belgium were all racing against time to secure whatever concessions they could obtain to frustrate any rival's hopes of achieving a complete monopoly.

Driven by its very momentum, the competition of the powers kept on moving into higher gear. Great Britain, France and Japan, alarmed by growing competition, moved to prevent the cession to anyone else of regions where their trade was particularly promising. In this way, in 1898, Great Britain obtained a pledge relating to the six provinces bordering on the Yangtze River; France, to the three Southern provinces and to Hainan island; and Japan, to the coastal provinces of Fukien. So, before the century came to its end, ten of the eighteen provinces south of the Great Wall were included in the 'spheres of interest' of these three powers. In addition there was already the German sphere in Shantung, and the Russian privileges in three provinces in Manchuria. Clearly, China had no chance to play off one power against the other. In league with Japan, they dissected China in unison.

Thus, within a few years after the Treaty of Shimonoseki, to all intents and purposes, China was carved up for political influence, for economic penetration, and for railway building. Unmistakably, the stage was set for the next phase, for the actual dismemberment of the country.

The apparently inevitable advance towards partition, however, was suddenly checked by a newcomer on the world stage.

Through the annexation of the Philippines, the United States had just become a major power in the Pacific, able to make her influence felt in the Far East. This new position of strength made it possible to safeguard American commercial interests in China; interests already threatened by the exclusive rights of various powers within their respective 'spheres of influence'. The new American policy was set forth in 1899 in a series of notes to the Treaty Powers. Secretary of State Hay asked them to refrain from monopolizing trade in their spheres and to preserve instead an Open Door for the trade of all nations.

So, America herself did not wish to impose legal disabilities on China. Nor did she condemn those who indulged in such practices. What the United States proposed was that the privileges which had been secured should not be monopolized by any one power but should be equally shared by all foreign traders. Assurances were demanded, however, on some essential points. 'Spheres of influence', for example, should not affect the treaty rights of other nations. The collection of customs duty should remain in the hands of the Chinese authorities.

Finally, no preferential railway or harbour charges should benefit the traders of any power. Thus, the Open Door policy was a compromise formula for containing rivalry between the powers within limits. Yet the practical effect of the American demands—and, in particular, of the one which insisted that the collection of customs duty should remain in Chinese hands—was to arrest the process which probably would have led to the carving up of China into colonies.

Instead, what had been imperialism on individual account, was to become a procedure under which the Chinese were to be presented with joint, international claims. In fact, it was from this moment onward that the basic contradiction developed in United States policy in the Far East. If the United States was instrumental in checking Japan's imperialistic encroachments in China, simultaneously she had added her own weight to those of the western powers. On balance, China's territorial integrity survived, but at the cost of increased vulnerability in face of antagonists henceforth concerting their action.

It was in face of this new situation that the anger of the Chinese spilled over into violent action. The activities of foreigners had been steadily undermining the prestige of the dynasty. Military defeats had all but destroyed the Government's authority. The heavy indemnities imposed after each defeat put an ever growing share of the country's revenue under foreign control. Yet reluctant to take the final plunge and embark on partition, the foreign powers continued to prop up the Manchu Court, to maintain it just strong enough to be able to serve as their intermediary. The peasants whose expression of discontent was restricted to secret societies, were resentful both of hardships and of national humiliation. Secret societies, of course, were numerous and they were traditionally anti-dynastic. Under prevailing conditions they had become also anti-foreign.

The Society of Harmonious Fists—better known as the Boxers—was one of these secret societies. Passionate and uneducated, vindictive and superstitious, the movement was also

The Boxer
Rebellion

patriotic and popular. Foreigners, unaware of the temper and of the sense of humiliation of the masses, tended to under-estimate its strength. As for the Court, seeing the spread of the movement, it attempted a diversionary gamble. To blunt its anti-dynastic aims, the Manchus offered to support its anti-foreign content. In the North in particular, looting and anti-foreign violence were widespread. Large numbers of missionaries and Chinese converts had been murdered and all the sufferings of China had been blamed on the 'foreign devils'. By January 1900 the Boxer rebellion had gained considerable popular strength. Orthodox Chinese opinion considered it with the respect due to a genuine patriotic movement and it was rendered the more respectable by the Court's barely concealed support. By the summer, all foreigners resident in Peking found themselves besieged within the hastily fortified Legation Quarter.

With the security of their citizens in China in danger, not to mention their prestige, the powers hastily organized an inter-national military expedition. Advancing from the coast, it soon occupied Peking. But neither in looting, nor in the savagery or the volume of the atrocities committed, was the invaders' performance inferior to that of the men they had come to punish. Hundreds of the capital's inhabitants were driven to seek refuge in suicide.

Seeds of Decay

THE REBELLION WAS BROKEN. But the problem facing the triumphant powers was once again whether to bring down the imperial government or whether they should content themselves by punishing it while prolonging its existence as their helpless but indispensable tool. Interest dictated the latter course. Nevertheless, a cruel and humiliating peace—the Boxer Protocol—was imposed.

Amongst a variety of penalties, the severe punishment of offenders was ordered, many of them by death. Foreign garrisons were to be quartered permanently in the capital itself for the defence of the Legations. Foreign troops were to police communications between Peking and the sea. The Taku forts, guarding the capital, were to be destroyed. And as usual, China was also to pay a heavy indemnity, offering the foreigners still greater control over the country's revenues; an indemnity of over a hundred million pounds (later somewhat reduced), a share of which was to be turned over to the missionaries. Moreover, in towns where foreigners had been harmed, the imperial examinations for admission to the higher ranks of the civil service were suspended for five years; a measure designed to improve the chances of young men educated by Christian missionaries.

The triumph of repression by superior arms was total. The Court reverted to its previous role of subservience. The West's authority in China was once again uncontested. The missions achieved near-monopoly of education. The gunboats on the Yangtze continued to maintain order and to inspire fear. The decisive levers of China's economy were controlled by western interests. And it was hardly surprising if, in the glow of their satisfaction and self-confidence, few westerners in the country noted that underneath the imposed order, profound and far-reaching changes were coming over China.

To begin with, following the Boxer Protocol, the foundation

The Manchu
Dynasty

19

The Chinese Revolution

stone of the established order, the Manchu Dynasty itself, was clearly doomed.

With the final decadence of the Ming Dynasty, by the middle of the seventeenth century, time was ripe for another change. Once again peasants were rising in rebellion and in the ensuing turmoil, a new dynasty imposed itself. Though relying on mixed legions—composed of Chinese, Manchu, Mongol and Korean troops—the main elements of Manchu government, whether in the field of taxation or of administration, were essentially Chinese. But ever since 1644 the Manchu rulers had been considered a foreign dynasty and, perhaps for this same reason, their deliberate policy had been to represent themselves as guardians of orthodox Chinese traditions. Though they had become thoroughly Chinese, and under their best Emperors China had known periods of both material and cultural flowering, anti-Manchu sentiment remained a decisive ingredient of Chinese nationalism.

Nevertheless, the dynasty successfully weathered the secret conspiracies and the numerous rebellions which had punctuated its rule up to the middle of the nineteenth century. Had it not been for the Manchus' inability to resist the foreigners, they would probably have merged into the flow of Chinese history. As it happened, the decay of the dynasty coincided with a very special chapter in China's history; with the period when, for the first time, it was becoming interdependent with that of the rest of the world.

In fact, from the Opium War onward the Manchu Dynasty had become the prisoner of an insoluble contradiction. It had to be strong enough to make China bend to the foreigners' will, yet sufficiently weak to be unable to resist their exactions. Resentment against the system of imperialist exploitation thus inevitably stirred anti-dynastic passions. And all during this crucial period fortune had placed supreme power in the hands of a corrupt and ignorant woman whose personality fatally marked China's evolution from 1860 till her death in 1908.

Yehomala, better known as the Dowager Empress Tzu Hsi (or the Old Buddha) was the daughter of a Manchu nobleman.

As the first-class concubine of the Emperor and mother of the heir-apparent, she had been in a position to assume full powers on the death of the ruler in 1860. When she became the effective Regent, the Taiping rebellion was not yet over. Other outbreaks were to follow. Yet during those critical years the personality of the Dowager Empress appeared particularly well suited to the ambivalent and painful phase through which China had been passing.

She had a domineering and unscrupulous personality. Her taste for Court intrigue was allied with an uncanny ability to strike down friend and foe alike whenever her interests so demanded. Yet there was superficial stability and prosperity under her reign. Isolated attempts at reform were quickly abandoned under the pressure of orthodox officials fearful of change. But the lack of principles and the taste for luxury of the Dowager Empress herself; corruption and the general and prodigious waste of the State's funds; the domination of the Court by debased eunuchs and a pleasure-loving horde of demoralized officials; all this deprived the Court of any pretence to leadership in a period of rapid change. Already totally discredited and cut off from popular opinion, the dynasty entered on its phase of final decay after the Boxer rebellion. Paradoxically, the resigned servility of the Dowager Empress gave the last years of her rule a quaint air of dignified tranquillity. Also, for a short while, the Russo-Japanese war protected China from the usual attentions of the western powers. This way, long before her death in 1908, the Manchu Dynasty had practically ceased to interest the world. The boy Pu Yi, who succeeded the Old Buddha, hardly counted any longer. By then it was obvious that he would have no throne to mount by the time he would be old enough to rule.

But the rotting away of the Manchu Dynasty was only one, perhaps the least significant, aspect of the awakening of China. In the background there had been structural changes and new intellectual trends, all seeking political expression. Reluctant for decades, at last China was beginning to react to the challenge of the outside world.

Population
and
economic
pressures

The Chinese Revolution

Perhaps none of these changes was more compelling than the rapid growth of the country's population and the beginning of the transformation in its economic structure.

Believed to have been around 100,000,000 by the middle of the seventeenth century, China's population quadrupled during the following two hundred years. In the course of the nineteenth century the pressure of the population on the land was becoming irresistible. The traditional methods of repression were no longer adequate to cope with peasant revolts. Inevitably, then, changes were needed in the country's economic structure itself. In that field, however, China's experience had not been very different from that of the other lands which had come under the West's economic influence.

The intrusion of a mercantile economy, combined with a monopoly of maritime trade and enforced against a predominantly agrarian society, invariably produced the same results. Like a giant magnet it drew the ancient centres of economic gravity toward coastal trading points. There, the materially superior foreigner bought the natives' products and gave in exchange his own industrial goods. It was this same process which had undermined the Moghul Empire in India and the native Kingdoms of South-east Asia.

The growth of the ports   In the ports where the foreigner had gained a foothold, a class of intermediaries emerged. Its economic and political ambitions had inevitably become intertwined with those of the foreigners. As a result, the seats of dynamic power began to shift from the central and provincial capitals to the newly prosperous ports. Like Bombay, Madras or Calcutta in India; Rangoon in Burma; or Haiphong and Saigon in Viet Nam, so in China, cities like Canton, Hankow, Shanghai or Tientsin emerged as the new centres of vital activity. They were assuming this role at the expense of the former, inland seats of trade, industry and learning. And the shift, of course, involved in each case a fundamental change in power relationships within the country. Moreover, the men personifying the dynamism of the new centres were inevitably the most receptive to the ideas, the methods and to the way of living of the foreigners whose intervention had been at the origin of their promotion.

During the last decades of the nineteenth century, the coastal areas where foreigners had established their authority in China, had become veritable nurseries of a new way of life. About half a dozen ports had become the centres of the new economic and financial power. Though real control was in European hands, Chinese intermediaries—conducting trade between the interior and the foreigners—were gradually acquiring important stakes. The order and security assured within the foreign enclaves tended to encourage enterprise and thus to attract Chinese skill and capital. Again, the educational opportunities provided—by missionaries, through study abroad, or simply as a result of contact with the foreigners' ideas and skills —only accelerated the trend.

This way, gradually, a new class of Chinese was beginning to emerge. Under the shield of foreign influence at the beginning, it was growing increasingly detached from the ideas and the way of living of the immense majority of Chinese. What is more, the Chinese who had become associated with western enterprise in their own country, were soon aspiring to perform the role all alone. Indeed, the growth of Chinese capitalism had been rapid. From 1865 onward Chinese enterprise and industry had been making important strides. Shipping companies and banks had been founded and the first consumer goods industries were making their appearance in the big cities. There was the beginning of shipbuilding in Shanghai. And the new industrialists and the entrepreneurs, envious of western privileges, became the natural allies of the emerging modern nationalist.

The Chinese had no difficulty in convincing themselves that they were not less able to organize modern enterprise than were foreigners. Then, Japan's swift victory over Russia administered a timely blow to the white man's prestige in Asia. Simultaneously, the various boycott movements, strikes and demonstrations, further proved that China's rising class of young intellectuals had unlimited possibilities to provide

A new class

23

accumulating political passion with organized and ideological expression.

Westernization   But in addition to these structural changes, other forces also helped to sponsor new ideas and worked for westernization. Missionary education, students returning from study abroad, and the influence of the overseas Chinese were perhaps the most important among them.

Though far from frequently, individual Chinese had occasion to obtain degrees at western or at Japanese universities. Some of them indeed played prominent roles in the reform movements toward the end of the nineteenth century. The first governmental attempt to send students abroad, dates from 1872 when a group of thirty students left for America. Up to 1875 all the 120 planned for the period had left, but the scheme could not be continued because of the opposition of the bureaucratic and scholarly *élite*. But in the meantime, in 1865, a school was established in Peking intended to supply foreign language interpreters to the Government. Gradually, this institute grew into a college teaching also scientific subjects. Yet these isolated experiments apart, modern education in China remained almost exclusively in the hands of missionaries.

While Catholic missionaries had been active in China from the early fourteenth century, Protestant missionaries did not reach the country until 1807. Then, with the opening up of the interior of the country, the number of missionaries active in China increased fast. In the course of the nineteenth century the number of Chinese Catholics is believed to have grown to half a million and that of the Protestants to over fifty thousand. But with their religion, the missionaries also brought their educational system. They were responsible also for the beginnings of modern medicine in China. Even if the West's religion and culture were striking at the roots of Chinese civilization, and even if the missionary effort in China was not without objectionable features, missionary schools were primarily responsible for bringing knowledge of the outside world to at least a minority of the Chinese. The great colleges of western learning in Shanghai and elsewhere, run by Christian missionaries, were beginning to offer China men and women of modern education. Then, too, the considerable amount of western material translated into Chinese by the missionaries, was by no means all on religious subjects. In fact, even elementary notions of modern science or western techniques and of the scientific approach in general, had first penetrated China through the Christian schools.

Another factor that powerfully contributed to the breakdown of the old order was the influence of the Chinese communities living outside the country.

The overseas Chinese

They were composed of descendants of Chinese who had emigrated or had been hired to work abroad. As usual they were industrious and frugal and the first thing they had wanted to buy with their money had been education for their children so that they should succeed even better. Their role in the Chinese Revolution had been decisive both because of their financial contribution and because they communicated ideas which helped to orientate and to shape Chinese political thinking. If the new *bourgeoisie* in the Treaty Ports acted like the leaven of modernization inside the country, Chinese communities abroad powerfully reinforced that role from the outside.

Those established in Hong Kong, under British rule, had regular ties with their families left behind in China. In at least the adjacent province of Kwangtung, such contacts undoubtedly helped to convey a view of the outside world not otherwise available to the Empire's subjects. From farther away, but on a far larger scale, the same kind of influence was exerted by Chinese communities living in South-east Asia, in the Philippines, Hawaii, or even in the United States. Although tenaciously clinging to their national characteristics, these communities benefited by foreign education and had long contact with other civilizations. All this could not fail to convince these patriotic expatriates of the necessity of reforms and changes in their country of origin. That in most cases they were experiencing the vulnerability of a minority, must only have strengthened their desire to see their mother-country progress and be prosperous and strong. Thus, it is not surprising that those advocating change at home have often found their most fervent supporters among Chinese abroad.

Yet notwithstanding these developments, so long as the Empire lasted and the imperial institutions withstood change, the movement for modernization could make no decisive progress. The minority exposed to western influences remained an alien body within the nation. Its ideas had found no echo in the mass of the people whose life and thinking were still governed by habit and tradition. And the Empire's administrative structure, its educational system, as much as the mental processes they had helped to perpetuate, ensured that the influence of the reformers should be firmly circumscribed by the Empire's scholarly and bureaucratic *élite*.

The System of Government

THE GOVERNMENTAL SYSTEM that had prevailed in China for countless centuries, had been unique both in its spirit and in its practice. A country more populous than any other in the world had been held together by an autocratic monarchy relying on the bureaucracy of scholarly officials. They had enjoyed the profound respect of the masses to whom their learning was a symbol of a unified national culture. And it was that culture which, for many centuries, had marked off the Chinese from everyone else. In fact, for about a thousand years the methods and rules, and the cultural and social content of that system of government, had remained virtually unchanged.

Government which shaped the daily life of the peasant masses was local both in its origin and in its application. Above it, political unity was ensured by the unified governmental system and cultural unity of the huge areas was preserved by the ideographic script. It rendered not sounds but ideas adaptable to place and to local circumstances. And this cultural unity has repeatedly saved China from the spiritual fragmentation that had regularly beset vast empires.

The guardians of this cultural unity had been the persons learned in the art of writing and in the traditions handed down from the remote past. They had been the principal administrators and the local governors who represented the imperial authority. To read the documents of the past and to write the records of present proceedings were indispensable instruments of authority. Those who mastered these complicated skills—involving the memorization and the interpretation of thousands of ideographs—were inevitably few. Yet instead of being an obstacle to efficient government, such virtual monopoly of learning by a small minority rather tended to facilitate ideological control. It even helped to create a unifying solidarity among those who had a stake in the preservation of both order and of their own privileged status.

True, the scholar bureaucrats constituted a class. But they never became a caste. Their ranks always remained open to anyone capable of passing the required examinations in classics and in literature. In the cities, each year, young men had entered the rows of wooden booths in which the civil service examinations had been given. Indeed, it was this possibility that rendered the system tolerable. It permitted the promotion into the ruling group of men of even modest origin but of great ability who, otherwise, might have drifted to swell the ranks of violent opposition. This was of considerable importance.

But the imperial examinations stressed memorization of classical texts and the mastery of a refined literary style. They offered no technical education and even less the art of organization able to wield power. As late as the nineteenth century orthodox classical education did not include even elementary arithmetic. In contrast, it offered command of the general civic morality embedded in the classical texts. In fact, the propagation of this morality among the mass of the people was the central task of the educated minority. In this way, quotations of appropriate classical maxims, skill in the use of words, and reliance on subjective interpretation, have come to inspire the actions and to characterize the mental processes of China's ruling bureaucracy. Yet, as a whole, training of this kind kept rigorously apart material implementation and the importance attached to values and ideals.

It is this background which helps to explain the bureaucrat-scholar class's strange reaction to its encounter with the West. A system which had worked so well in the past depended on the maintenance of the traditional ideology. At all cost it had to be shielded from the corroding influence of intruding foreign ideas. And the opposition went to absurd lengths. As old patterns of war-making had usually sufficed to put down rebellion, the mandarins remained unimpressed even by the uncanny efficiency of western arms, even though they had repeated opportunity to experience their disastrous force. Only unshakeable faith in their system, one that had guaranteed a millennium of stability, could explain such suicidal obstinacy in refusing to admit the need for change. And in retrospect, it is the astonishing rigidity of these mental processes which seem so decisively to have determined the course China's revolution was to take.

At some point in the course of the nineteenth century every corner of the non-western world had found itself before a painful choice. Either it had to submit to western domination and to accept a colonial or semi-colonial status, or it had to assimiliate enough of western technology and organizational methods to be able to repel western aggression. China was no exception. But it is one of the most extraordinary chapters of modern history how and why China failed to take up the challenge. In trying to understand what had happened to China during the past half century, one may as well begin by asking why China did not react to the Opium War the way Japan reacted to the somewhat impetuous presentation of Commodore Perry's visiting card?

China rejects the western challenge

The answer, or a great deal of the answer, must have been in the peculiar social and administrative structure of the country. Feudal power, based on land, was important on the local level but was ineffective against the imperial authority. That authority, on the other hand, depended primarily on the mandarins and on their position in the administrative structure. The group which dominated, owed its cohesion and its authority not to wealth but to the successful enforcement of a single official ideology. It was orthodox Confucianism and education was synonymous with indoctrination in that official ideology. Thus anyone qualified to administer or to lead, automatically must have been a supporter of the official system. If in nineteenth-century Japan feudal power was independent enough to experiment with western technology, no such enterprise was imaginable in China without the support and the lead of the scholar officials.

To admit western technology and organization, however, would have meant for them the sharing of their powers with people whose education and habits of thought would have been completely different from theirs. It would have involved not merely the dilution of their power, but also a conscious abdication of the prestige of classical learning to which the mandarins owed much of their authority.

Tradition prepares its own destruction

In Japan, it was possible for a section of the ruling group to admit new ideas without endangering its own position. That position was not dependent on the prestige of one particular ideology. But not so in China. There, timely readjustment to the coming challenge had been short-circuited by the hold of orthodoxy. And its inability to face realities, left the satisfaction of the need for progress to the revolutionaries.

In practice, the degree of a leader's attachment to the traditional system was inversely proportionate to his ability to sponsor China's inevitable westernization. If she wanted to progress, China needed western science, technology, and western methods of organization. The longer the guardians of China's traditional civilization refused to admit at least these indispensable components of progress, the more they prepared the ground for the revolutionary's intent to destroy the traditional system as a whole.

Stepping back, as it were, for a panoramic view of the China at the end of the last century, these, then, were the forces at work.

The overwhelming mass of the people continued to exist within the framework of the ancient and unchanging moral order. Missionary education apart, little if any outside influence disturbed the structure. And wherever that outside influence touched small minorities, it could be discredited owing to its alien origin. Yet in the tiny enclaves of modern economy, planted on Chinese soil by foreigners, new ideas were striking roots. A new class of Chinese was arising, aware of the paralysing impact of the old system. To them it was clear not only that the West had left China behind in the march of human progress, but also that Japan, herself westernized, could dictate terms to her giant Chinese neighbour. The restlessness caused by this awakening was powerfully reinforced by the education dispensed by foreigners, by students returning from abroad, as well as by the urgings of the Chinese communities abroad.

The System of Government

Put together, these scattered minorities constituted a modest power-house of new ideas. Facing them was the monolithic immobility of traditional Chinese society. It was the problem how to transmit this new energy to the masses that needed solution. And that role was to be performed by China's emerging generation of young intellectuals.

Chinese history had produced numerous literary monuments of self-criticism, or critical analysis, or of a questioning of the prevailing system. But notwithstanding decades of national humiliation, the renaissance of liberal and rationalist ideas in modern China was surprisingly late. When it came at last, it was confused. It suffered numerous setbacks and repeatedly appeared to succumb to obstruction before its full impact could have been felt. Men of searching intellect or of liberal ideas were not lacking. Only the receptivity of the country seemed to be at fault. The turning point seemed to have come with the shock of China's unexpected defeat by Japan. In the years following it several men of stature were beginning openly to advocate reform.

The Renaissance of ideas

Kang Yu-wei (1858–1927), a Cantonese historian, was one of them. Not a practising official, nevertheless he had some influence on certain circles connected with the Court. He had been impressed both by Japan's success in her attempt at westernization, and by the subjective authoritarianism which had been corrupting China's governing circles. For him constitutional monarchy offered the way out. Still under the impact of Japan's victory, in 1898, the Emperor—to whom the Dowager Empress temporarily yielded power—was willing to follow Kang's advice. Under his influence a number of changes were decided.

'Those who claim to be conservative patriots consider that all the old customs should be upheld and new ideas repudiated without compromise . . .' said the Emperor's first reform decree. '. . . If we continue to drift with our army untrained, our resources disorganized, our scholars ignorant and our artisans without technical training, how can we possibly hope to hold our own among the nations? . . .' Thus '. . . we now issue this special Decree so that all our subjects, from the Imperial family downwards, may hereafter exert themselves in the cause of reform. The basis of education will continue to rest on the canons of the sages, but at the same time there must be careful investigation of every branch of European learning appropriate to existing needs. . . .'

Reform and reaction

Action followed his words. The old examination system was abolished and new subjects were introduced into the curriculum. A quick succession of decrees projected modern colleges and schools, including a naval college, as well as mining and railway bureaux. A department for the translation of foreign publications too was to be established. And a number of useless, ceremonial posts were abolished. But this extraordinary attempt, so evidently inspired by Japan's example, alarmed the traditional scholar-bureaucrats. When Kang turned his attention to military and naval reform, he soon found that national control of the armed forces barely existed. In the meantime, however, the Dowager Empress had been alerted by the jealous officials and in the ensuing web of palace-intrigues Tzu Hsi resumed full power, deposed and imprisoned the reforming Emperor. Kang Yu-wei himself saved his life only by escaping to Hong Kong. And so, the promising interlude of 'the hundred days of reform' came to an abrupt end.

This abortive experience, however, did not put an end to the intellectual ferment. Inside the country or in exile, there were others calling for and working in the service of change. Some of them were what may be termed practical traditionalists. They were conscious of the need for reform but wished to bring it about within the established framework. They hoped to uphold the imperial institution and to bring about the transformation without any weakening of attachment to Confucian values. Others again, represented more radical views. To them Confucianism was of no further use and only a republican form of government could provide the constitutional frame to operate revolutionary changes.

Advocates of change

Around Kang Yu-wei several other prominent men stood for modernization without a break with the past. Liang Chi-chao, a Hunanese, had been associated with Kang in the hundred days' attempt and had the sympathy of several other scholars of his province. Like Kang, he too escaped after the Empress's *coup d'état* and continued his campaign from Japan. He insisted that China needed both new ideas and new ideals to turn the Chinese into 'a new people'. And the journal he edited in Japan had undoubtedly great influence on the younger generation who, later on, were to re-launch China's reform movement.

Some others, like the Viceroy Chang Chih-tung (1837–1909), worked in the same direction. He was a highly placed official and a successful administrator. He advocated the sending of Chinese students abroad and he believed also in the urgent necessity to open the Empire to western learning. But he wanted the material strength derived from the assimilation of western ways and means to strengthen the ancient moral order and to uphold both the dynasty and Confucianism. His advocacy of gradual change was succinctly expressed in an essay, published in 1898, and entitled *Learn!* It found a wide audience among the scholars still smarting under the humiliation of Shimonoseki, and had been distributed by order of the Emperor himself.

'. . . In order to render China powerful, and at the same time preserve our own institutions, it is absolutely necessary that we should utilize western knowledge. But unless Chinese learning is made the basis of education, and a Chinese direction given to thought, the strong will become anarchists, and the weak slaves. . . . The English newspapers have recently been ridiculing us for not reforming, and they state that the teachings of Confucius lie at the bottom of our inflexible conservatism. In this they are greatly mistaken . . .' he wrote in his essay. 'China received her first warning in Formosa when the aborigines rebelled, the second in the Liu Chieu Islands, the third in Ili, the fourth in Korea, the fifth in Annam and Burma, and the sixth in the Japanese war, and the country is now in extreme danger. The warnings have been sent by Heaven to open the eyes of the Chinese, and the Chinese officials and people elect to remain blind, stubborn, and proud as of old. What more can we say? . . .'

But the advocates of modernization were not numerous enough to impress the conservative mandarins or to create adequate popular pressure for change. Perhaps it was already too late. A number of other men of learning and of great reputation seemed to believe so. Accordingly, they preferred to advocate revolution rather than reform.

Sun Yat-sen

In his later years Liang Chi-chao himself abandoned his monarchism and joined the ranks of those calling for a Republic. Not surprisingly, however, there were very few scholar-officials among these early republicans. The most influential were either expatriates, writing from abroad, or men who grew up in the coastal areas subject to western trade influences. Some among them lived and worked in the safety of the foreign concessions. They had been influenced by missionaries or, as it happened quite often, had obtained financial aid from Chinese abroad. The one destined to play the most important role among them was Sun Yat-sen. He was, in fact, the living symbol of all these characteristics.

Sun Yat-sen (1866–1925) was born in the coastal area, the traditional source of Chinese emigrants. As a boy he had left for Hawaii where he studied in American schools. It was there that he was baptized a Protestant Christian. Later on he studied for a medical degree in Hong Kong and travelled widely in the United States, in Europe and in Asia. Most of his life was spent in revolutionary organization. For the Manchus, Sun was a marked man with a price on his head. His periods of exile were followed by years of clandestine activities in China, punctuated again by more or less prolonged retirement to the safety of foreign concessions. During all those years Sun Yat-sen had been, as it were, the liaison officer-number-one between China's revolutionary circles and politically minded Chinese abroad.

The first adherents to his revolutionary republican programme had naturally been recruited from among the middle classes. Frustrated by the reactionary immobility of Imperial China, they readily turned to his prescription of national rejuvenation. Here, then, was a leader not educated in classical Chinese learning but one who had spent much of his life abroad and who, unlike most of the reformers inside China, was familiar with western ideas, intellectual trends, and political techniques. Uninhibited by inherited respect either for Confucianism or for imperial institutions, he was, in a sense, the only true revolutionary among the personalities who had dominated the Chinese political scene during those formative years.

Under the influence of these men, what had begun as mere intellectual probings and the examination of the causes of national weakness, was beginning to take political forms. The relative freedom of the foreign settlements offered new opportunities for political organization. Indeed, they had gradually become veritable seats of a powerful nationalist movement, by then openly hostile to the Court. The middle-class intellectuals, as much as the budding proletariat of the big cities, were experimenting with new ideas and new methods. Well-organized and powerful boycott movements offered a foretaste of things to come. The new 'coastal' nationalism was beginning to spread toward the hitherto immobile interior. By the beginning of this century it seemed as if the problem of transmitting the energy of the tiny, intellectual power-house to the broad masses, was about to be solved. The activities of the various revolutionary groups and movements were beginning to bear fruit. They produced strikes, demonstrations, and even uprisings. Most of them, of course, were quickly crushed. Yet they were steadily gaining momentum.

The decisive one occurred in Wuchang on the evening of 10 October 1911—the Double Tenth, as it is now remembered. **The Double Tenth** Incensed by arbitrary arrests and executions, some of the imperial troops mutinied and besieged the Viceroy's offices. He promptly took refuge on a gunboat on the Yangtze River while the rebels proclaimed their aim to overthrow the Manchu Dynasty. Prudently enough, they also made it clear that it was their purpose to protect foreigners and their property so as to diminish the danger of foreign intervention.

35

The Chinese Revolution

During the following days the rebellion spread to other cities. Within three days the rebels were in full control of the large urban conglomeration composed of Wuchang, Hankow and Hanyang on the two banks of the Yangtze and thus controlled Central China's principal centre of trade and communications.

Barely a month later most of the South, as well as some northern centres, came out unambiguously on the side of the revolutionaries. The chaotic weeks which followed culminated in a peace conference between republicans and government forces, held in Shanghai. Simultaneously, the various revolutionary factions had been meeting in Nanking and proceeded to adopt a republican constitution. Sun Yat-sen, just returned from abroad, reached Shanghai on December 24 and five days later was elected Provisional President of the Republic. On New Year's day he arrived in Nanking and took oath first to obtain the abdication of the Manchus and then to resign so as to permit the election of the first President of the Republic.

In the meantime, somewhat belatedly, the Court hurriedly accepted the inauguration of a constitutional monarchy and appointed Yuan Shih-kai as its first Prime Minister. For long a devoted servant of the Manchus, he had gained complete control over the Court and had thus become the natural choice to negotiate with the republicans once it became clear that the Court's reforms had come too late. Negotiations between Sun Yat-sen and General Yuan Shih-kai led finally to a decree which declared that under suitable guarantees the dynasty would abdicate. On 12 February 1912—four months after the Double Tenth—the formal abdication took place.

The end of
Imperial China

So, after 267 years the rule of the Manchu Dynasty came to an end. With it went also the system of imperial government which had been in existence for over two thousand years.

The temptation was great to believe that 10 October 1911, marked the triumph of a long movement of liberation. In reality, it marked only the final collapse of a civilization incapable of adapting itself to the needs of a rapidly changing world.

36

Part Two

The Republic in the Balance

ON 13 FEBRUARY 1912, Peking and the other big cities of China were all quiet. The news of the end of the monarchy was well received. Vigorous proclamations had been posted on the gates of the capital and they recommended calm and threatened trouble-makers with capital punishment. But this was barely necessary. Life was going on as usual.

Outwardly the old order was gone and in its place a new, republican edifice was being erected. But behind the façade the revolution was merely beginning to search for the content of its coming, constructive phase. For the time being there were vague intentions only. They were barely enough to fill the vacuum created by the collapse of the dynastic order.

After a century of foreign aggression and the intrusion of alien ideas, China was enmeshed in a network of imposed obligations, financial commitments, and of humiliating controls. Now central government had practically ceased to exist. Taking hold of the debris of authority, the viceroys and the governors of the provinces were assuming independent powers.

Traditional religious beliefs had been undermined both by the imported rationalism and by the long-protected activities of Christian missionaries. The ideology which used to govern the actions of individuals and the State had been discredited by continuous attacks on Confucian doctrines. Then, the pillars of the old order had been removed one by one. The civil service examinations had been abolished. Hereditary monarchy was discarded. Then the traditional pattern of the schools was giving way to a new kind of education including western subjects. In the meantime, the traders and the goods of the West had gradually destroyed the country's traditional, self-centred economy. In its place there emerged a distorted structure whose levers were controlled either from abroad or from the handful of foreign enclaves enjoying extra-territorial privileges on Chinese soil.

39

The Chinese Revolution

The western ideas which had been flooding into China appeared to be incompatible with China's inherited institutions and inapplicable to the country's historical experience. Yet, notwithstanding the will to learn, genuine curiosity, or even hard thinking, few had precise ideas how to bring a democratic republic about and how to make it work. Like matter in a reactor after a century of pitiless bombardment, Chinese culture and civilization lay disintegrated like an atomized, inchoate mass. Its identity lost, it was as yet unable to find its new composition.

Thus, inevitably perhaps, for some years more China's revolution continued along its destructive course before the outlines of its positive content could emerge. And in the meantime, more than once, it seemed as if even the practical achievements of the Double Tenth would have to be sacrificed.

Ending the civil war

Following the abdication of the Manchus the most urgent task was to put an end to the civil war. To further that aim Sun Yat-sen—Provisional President of the improvised Revolutionary National Assembly at Nanking—retired in favour of Yuan Shih-kai. The Imperial Party had confidence in him and he commanded what was still the strongest army in the country. But in order to appease the contending factions, Yuan would have needed much subtlety and exceptional qualities of statesmanship. Unfortunately for China he was ill-armed with such tools of compromise. In fact, it became soon evident that he had no great faith in the Republic and that his personal ambition commanded all other considerations.

The South, as a whole, was republican and stood for the democratization of institutions. The Kuomintang, or the Nationalist Party, was the best organized expression of this sentiment and its representatives dominated the Nanking Assembly. By contrast, in the North of the country the conservative forces appeared to be the stronger and over large areas actual power was in the hands of military men. They were by no means enthusiasts for the republican idea.

As for the foreign powers, still the prime movers of the country's fate, their attitude was prudent and ambiguous. They were not decided to oppose the Republic. Nor were they more inclined than in the past to encourage the emergence of really popular institutions able to rely on mass backing. So, instinctively, their preference went to the encouragement of a 'strong man'. In this way, in the struggle between the radical South, and the conservative forces behind Yuan Shih-kai, the weight of foreign influence was behind the latter.

Against the Assembly's will, Yuan transferred it to Peking. Barely a month after the abdication, a provisional constitution was promulgated on March 10. The National Assembly was elected in 1913 and the Kuomintang was dominant within it. Inevitably, friction between Parliament and the President grew intense. The major clash occurred over a loan offered by the six Great Powers. The treasury empty and Parliament in an obstructive mood, the loan of £25 million offered the President a convenient way out.

But the terms of the loan provoked considerable public indignation. It was to be advanced by a bankers' consortium— backed by Great Britain, France, Germany, Russia, Japan and the United States—on condition that no future loans were to be accepted from other countries and that the income from the salt gabelle was to serve as its guarantee. President Wilson, just elected, caused the USA to withdraw her participation as, in his view, the conditions attached to the loan menaced China's administrative independence. But the remaining five powers went ahead with the project. Yet the Assembly, on its part, refused to ratify it. So, Yuan Shih-kai decided to force it through. As a reaction, four southern provinces organized a punitive expedition in order to remove the President. Though with great difficulty, Yuan crushed the revolt, and its leaders— Sun Yat-sen among them—fled to Japan. There, embittered against the financial intrigues of the western powers, Dr Sun resumed his revolutionary activities with new vigour. His faith in western liberalism, however, had received a blow from which it never recovered.

As for Yuan, the collapse of the South's revolt was the green light for him. In October 1913 he had himself elected President

Western financial intrigues

A new Emperor?

for five years. Soon after he expelled the Kuomintang representatives from the Assembly as a prelude to its coming dissolution. The next step was the creation of a bogus Parliament entrusted with the revision of the Constitution. Its first fruit was to give power to the President to prolong indefinitely his term of office and even to nominate his successor. Thus armed with absolute power, in 1915 Yuan Shih-kai went still further and decided to found a new dynasty. He had himself elevated to the throne under the regal title of Hung Hsien, meaning Glorious Constitutional Era.

At this moment, however, the renewed armed rebellion of southern republicans arrested the march of events. The movement was rapidly gathering momentum and in February 1916 the new Emperor felt obliged to announce the postponement of the actual enthronement. In another month the imperial retreat continued. In a decree he declared that he would continue his rule as mere President of the Republic. But the would-be Emperor's hesitations helped to encourage the republicans and, financial difficulties aiding, Yuan's power was beginning to decline. In June 1916 he died of a chronic disease aggravated, so it would seem, by chagrin. His Vice-President succeeded him and so the attempt to resurrect the monarchy was over.

No going back Another, still shorter tentative to restore the Confucian monarchy took place a year later. On 1 July 1917, the attempt was made to restore the boy-Emperor who had been deposed in 1912 as the last ruler of the Manchu Dynasty. Yet once again armed resistance frustrated the project. After only two weeks, the bewildered youngster, puppet of powerful political forces, was forced to retire again to his gilded refuge in Peking's imperial palace.

By this time, however, it was abundantly clear that the collapse of the monarchy had not prevented the age-old combination of landlords, scholars and military men from retaining much of their power. Yet the fiasco of the second attempt at restoration had demonstrated with equal clarity that the republican ideas had sufficient popular support to prevent a complete return to the old order. Clearly, then, China was unwilling to turn the clock back. Yet she did not quite know in what direction or how to advance. So, once again, external events and international forces were to intervene to help determine her course.

World War and its Aftermath

AFTER YUAN SHIH-KAI'S DEATH China's political dissolution continued. War-lords, or military strong men, took charge of different provinces leaving in Peking a central government with but nominal powers. It lived on the revenues of the customs administration and on the salt gabelle—under the control of foreign officials—while postal communications remained practically the sole symbol of national unity. This confusing situation was to last for no less than a full decade, until a political party commanded adequate military organization to attempt the reunification of the country.

In the meantime, the ground was being prepared. This was accompanied by intense rivalries between men and the ideas they stood for. As for the outside influences which have accelerated the process, they were connected with historic events such as the First World War, Japan's expansion overseas, and the Russian Revolution.

Noting that the war between the European powers was spreading, the Chinese were determined not to get involved. They declared their country's neutrality and even appealed to the USA to help them make their desire respected by the warring powers. But notwithstanding such precautions, inexorably, China found herself sucked into the global conflagration. This was due particularly to the activities of Japan.

The European powers being fully occupied with their war, Japan considered the occasion tempting. Though within the frame of the Anglo-Japanese alliance the British Government had attempted to limit Japanese intervention to mere local aid against German vessels in the Far East, Japan could not be restricted. To begin with, she wished to take over Germany's privileges in Shantung province. But while doing so, she also declared war on Germany and, very soon, Germans and Japanese were in battle on Chinese soil. As for the Chinese themselves, they looked on hopelessly just as they had done in

1905 when Japan had fought the Russians within China's borders. Yet all this was but the prelude of more drastic events.

A few months later, in January 1915, with the Powers still locked in war in Europe, and America's attention diverted across the Atlantic, Japan was ready for a bold move. The aim was no less than to establish her control over practically the whole of China. This was presented in the form of the celebrated Twenty-One Demands designed to procure for Japan both controlling and veto powers over China's military, financial and political activities. Intended by the Japanese to be kept secret, the content of the demands was 'leaked' by Chinese officials and became known in the United States. Thanks to the resulting American reaction, China could resist at least some of the claims. If they had all been granted, the Chinese Republic would have been transformed into a mere puppet of Japan. Under American pressure, Japan abandoned the more extreme demands. Yet many of them could not be resisted and China's assent was finally given on 9 May 1915.

Japan's twenty-one demands

As a matter of fact, the treaties in question were never ratified by the Chinese Parliament. For the same reason Chinese opinion went on considering them as not binding on their Government. Yet Japan's attempts to impose the treaties, and China's efforts to resist her claims, provided the central theme for the next twenty years of Sino-Japanese relations.

Meanwhile, as German pressure on the Allies increased, so also grew China's involuntary involvement in the First World War. To obtain Japanese naval help in the Mediterranean, and persuade her to put pressure on China to break off relations with Germany, Great Britain, France and Russia concluded a secret agreement with Japan. It promised to support at the coming peace conference the Japanese claim to the German holdings in Shantung province, as well as to the German Pacific islands north of the Equator. Simultaneously, America's growing involvement in the war exerted pressure in the same direction. When, in April 1917, the United States declared war on Germany, China was strongly urged to follow suit. After that, the decision could not be postponed much longer.

The Chinese Revolution

The Assembly, reconvened in Peking after the death of Yuan Shih-kai and dominated again by the Kuomintang, was at the time opposed to China's entry into the war. This was prompted by the fear that participation in it would provide Japan with further opportunities to extend and to consolidate her influence in China. But the Peking Government, backed by military commanders who controlled several provinces, stood for Chinese participation. In the ensuing manœuvring several northern provinces declared their independence of Peking, Parliament was dissolved and, in July 1917, the second attempt was made to restore the monarchy. Finally, what survived as the Central Government, and was considered as such by the Powers, declared war on Germany and Austria on 14 August 1917.

The first consequence was further division within the country and, in particular, the Kuomintang's dissent. Hostile to the northern war-lords who had supported the declaration of war, and considering the dissolution of Parliament as unconstitutional, the Kuomintang leaders withdrew to Canton. There they constituted what, in their view, was the sole legal government of the Chinese Republic. The constitutional basis of this southern government was the Parliament elected in 1913. For a while Sun Yat-sen himself participated in it but due to the usual friction with dissenting factions, he once again retired to the foreign concessions of Shanghai. There he continued his political and literary work, waiting for a more favourable political constellation.

As those who had opposed the declaration of war had correctly foreseen, Japanese control over China was growing rapidly. The country was divided and the treasury almost empty. The men who ruled at Peking soon had to turn to Japan for financial and other assistance. In exchange Peking had to offer still greater privileges in the exploitation of China's forests and mines, and still wider control over the country's railways, its telegraph system, and even over its tax structure. Fully occupied with her war effort against the Central Powers, rather than to alleviate China's dependence on Japan, the

46

United States even concluded an agreement with her in which she recognized Japan's 'special interests' in China. While it contained the admission that 'territorial propinquity creates special relations' between Japan and China, it also reaffirmed that China's territorial sovereignty ought not be impaired.

Though without any effective central government, China was assured a seat at the Versailles peace conference as one of the belligerents. Composed of representatives of both the Peking and the Canton Governments, the Chinese delegation was unanimous in asking for the abrogation of the 1915 and the 1918 Sino-Japanese treaties with all their imposed humiliations, as well as for the return of the former German properties in Shantung province. The first demand was considered as outside the scope of the peace conference. As for the second claim, Japan invoked her secret agreement with the Allies. Finally, the former German properties were awarded to Japan in conformity with the promise made to her during the war.

Anger at Allied betrayal

The decision provoked an outburst of anti-western feeling in China. It set off a series of violent demonstrations. Thus backed by public sentiment at home, the Chinese delegation refused to sign the Treaty of Versailles. Later on, however, in a separate Treaty, negotiated between China and Germany, the latter's extra-territorial privileges were renounced (as were also those of Austria), and so the dismantling of the 'unequal treaties' had begun. But this very partial triumph barely lessened the very widespread indignation caused by the Allies' attitude. In fact, the Versailles decisions helped more than anything else to galvanize nationalist sentiment. On 4 May 1919, Peking witnessed a mass demonstration by students whose example was followed all over the country. The effervescence so created, and probably reinforced by the violent anti-imperialist propaganda emanating from Moscow, provided convincing proof that Chinese nationalism was growing into a powerful force. Indeed, a series of demonstrations and boycott movements of unsuspected violence left no doubt that the war and its aftermath had powerfully helped to bring the masses within the revolutionary movement.

The Tide Turns

To be strong and united and to put an end to the foreigners' privileges in China, have always been the basic aims of the revolutionary movement. To achieve all this meant to give at last positive content to the revolution which had begun in 1911. The First World War, having shattered the foundations of the prevailing global order, appeared to have provided just the opportunity to do so. Yet to awaken the forces of constructive nationalism, so it seemed, China had to pass through still greater anarchy. And nothing could more cruelly illustrate the futility of that period than the power and the influence of the war-lords.

For about a decade after the death of Yuan Shih-kai real power in China had been in the hands of local military leaders, the *tu-chun* or the war-lords. Some were former officials or military governors, or had simply come up from the peasantry. Others again were just bandits who had managed to consolidate their power over more or less large areas. What characterized them all was command over a private army paid out of taxes extracted from the peasantry. War-lords, as a rule, bargained their support for or against rivals, or for or against the Central Government, though always with the ultimate aim to establish their own supremacy over all the others.

The war-lords

Those favoured by geography tried to gain control of a sea-port so as to be able to import arms. The less lucky ones, deeper inland, either had to purchase their arms or, in some cases, tried to set up an arsenal where they could manufacture them. The basic pattern, of course, was not new. A comparable situation had usually followed the decay of dynasties. But the situation after 1911 was different in many ways.

Both the armies and the weapons at the command of these 'modern' war-lords were more powerful than they had been in the past and, to that extent, they caused proportionately more suffering and greater devastation. Secondly, in view of the

Foreign support

49

The Chinese Revolution

Powers' deep involvement in China's affairs, most war-lords had direct or indirect dealings with a number of foreign governments. In practice, Japan and the western powers had each pursued distinct policies towards the war-lords. As usual, the western powers had been in search of a war-lord who could be built up as the uncontestable strong man; capable both of guaranteeing past agreements and eventually of mortgaging still more of the country's natural resources in return for financial aid. Not so Japan. It was not in her interest to have a strong and unified Chinese neighbour and, accordingly, she usually negotiated with and supported several rivals. In this way, normally, Japan obtained concessions from a regional war-lord, weakened him by supporting his opponents and, simultaneously, pressed for the recognition of the privileges thus obtained by the nominal Central Government of China.

Although occasionally the war-lords combined their forces and there had even been isolated moves toward federation among some of them, national unification remained a remote prospect. Some war-lords, like, for example, Chang Tso-lin who ruled Manchuria from 1911, were relatively honest men (the reason why he was finally eliminated by the Japanese who had his train blown up), while others participated in the aimless series of civil wars for no higher ideal than to further their personal and material ambitions.

But, inevitably, he who paid the bill was the Chinese peasant. Intermittent fighting and the cruelty and hunger that came with it, provided the permanent background of his daily existence. His son was carried off to make war and much of his produce was taken away in taxes. Such arbitrariness in everyday life turned him into an exhausted and dispirited man. His refuge was in a silent but passionate nationalism, easily diverted against the activities of foreigners in his country. Far above his head, the kaleidoscopic political changes kept on producing more or less ephemeral governments. There was a nominal President in Peking while in Canton, in April 1921, Sun Yat-sen was elected 'President of China' by the remnants of the 1913 Parliament. Nor did events beyond China's borders greatly help to bring to an end the anarchy within them. If war in the West came to an end, it continued to spread insecurity in East Asia for another four years because of Japan's attempts to occupy part of Siberia. While Europe was beginning to settle down in its new, post-war shape, the Far Eastern situation remained dangerously unstable. More and more clearly there was basic opposition between the Japanese and the Anglo-American concepts of the East Asia they wished to see emerge. But what really was at stake was the future of China.

The antagonisms were sufficiently powerful to lead to a race in naval armaments. To lessen its dangers was the primary purpose of the Washington Conference of 1921–22. By definition it met to limit naval armaments in the Pacific. In actual fact, it drew up new treaties intended to define the balance of naval and political power in the Far East.

The
Washington
Conference

The nine powers with direct interests in the area (the Soviet Union was not present) agreed 'to respect the sovereignty, the independence, and the territorial and administrative integrity of China'. But if Japan thus accepted the Anglo-American policy of the Open Door—of equal opportunity and of no special privileges in China—the naval agreements concluded at Washington seemed to annul the alignment so obtained. In fact, Japan was accorded what seemed to be a free hand to build up her naval supremacy in the Far East and so virtually to dominate the sea approaches to the Chinese coasts.

But in spite of these ambiguities, in a sense, the Washington Conference represented the beginning of the dismantling of foreign privileges in China. Japan was at last obliged to return her holdings in Shantung and to abandon at least the most obnoxious of the Twenty-One Demands. Moreover, China had raised a number of questions connected with limitations on her sovereignty, the liquidation of extra-territorial privileges in particular, and obtained the promise that her demands might be considered when internal conditions in the country (as well as many other pre-conditions) warranted such a step.

In spite of her chronic disunity, her domestic weakness, and the absence of any effective central authority, China thus

A changed
status

obtained substantial diplomatic gains whatever the ulterior motives of the powers may have been. Though in reality the country was still divided into about a dozen virtually separate entities, after the Washington Conference China was no longer menaced by actual dissolution. Rather the contrary. For the first time China had emerged as an accuser of the imperialist powers and, ideologically at any rate, forced them on the defensive. All this was a striking illustration of the vastly changed position of the western powers just emerging from the blood-letting of the First World War. But it was also an implied compliment paid by the rest of the world to the pressure of the rising tide of Chinese nationalism.

After the West's long monopoly of world power, new, non-occidental centres of power were emerging. China was among the first to benefit from the coming dispersal of world power. That, in a nutshell, was the indirect effect of the Russian Revolution on the Far Eastern situation. And it would have been surprising indeed if China's increasingly articulate nationalism would not have shown its gratitude toward those who had brought about that change.

The Russian Revolution

IN CHINA, AS IN THE REST OF ASIA, the news of the October Revolution was greeted with a mixture of curiosity and enthusiasm. During the six years since the fall of the monarchy, chaos and inexperience had prevented the liberal democratic institutions taking roots. So, it was amidst the resulting disillusionment with both democracy and the West that the news of the Bolshevik Revolution arrived. What was more, it offered immediate advantages to China.

Right from the beginning, the new régime in Moscow was lavish in its verbal encouragements to the independence struggle of the Asian masses. Then, in 1919, the Communist Government announced its readiness to give up Russia's privileges in China. It offered to enter into negotiations in view of the renunciation of Russia's extra-territorial rights, to return territories taken from China by the Tsars, to cancel Russia's share in the Boxer indemnity, and to hand back full control over the Chinese Eastern Railway in North Manchuria. Though the actual implementation of some of these offers remained partial or led to prolonged negotiations, nonetheless they were without precedent in China's experience with foreigners. Understandably, their psychological impact was considerable.

The historical background of Sino-Russian relations itself helped to create a favourable Chinese disposition. Although during the years which had preceded the war between Russia and Japan, the Russians had joined the western nations in taking full advantage of China's weakness, after 1905 Tsarist governments had remained inactive in Chinese affairs. In fact, accidentally or by design, throughout the nineteenth century Russian policy in China differed from that of the western powers in several decisive ways.

Russia had never made war on China in order to acquire privileges. When she had expanded at the expense of territory

No traditional hostility

claimed by China, the areas involved had not constituted integral parts of the historical Chinese State. In Manchuria itself, the Tsars' aggressive policy had at least attempted to safeguard Peking's sovereignty. Russia had not been involved either in foreign missionary activities, in the forcing of opium on China, or in the so-called 'pig trade', the forcible transportation under inhuman conditions of Chinese workers to plantations and to mines abroad. Even at the time of China's greatest humiliation following the Boxer rising, Russia took up an independent attitude and managed not to be associated with the most resented outrages perpetrated by the western victors. Owing to all these circumstances the Chinese had never felt on the part of the Russians the systematic condescension that did so much to stimulate their feeling against foreigners. Obviously, then, the renunciation of privileges in 1919 and the proclamations emanating from Moscow, echoing the aspirations of Chinese nationalism, fell on fertile ground.

The Soviet
alternative

The anti-western challenge implicit in the Russian Revolution had undoubtedly lent moral strength to Asian nationalist movements. For long the aim of Chinese and of Asian nationalists in general had been essentially political: to gain freedom from foreign domination. The Soviet Union's mere existence helped to give this political nationalism new, social and economic objectives. All of a sudden the Achilles' heel of the western world had been exposed in the form of its economic vulnerability. Simultaneously, the West's hold on Asian minds had been rapidly weakened through the emergence of an alternative fount of principles and ideas. And as a result, China's nationalists were soon divided into protagonists of the two rival ways of modernization and emancipation.

Generally speaking, such were the ideas and the stimulants behind China's unexpected tenacity at the Washington Conference. Yet they offered merely a foretaste of the immense strength of the gathering popular movement calling for an end to humiliation, to anarchy, and to dependence.

Popular
sentiment

At around the same time a series of events came to show that China was at last feeling her way toward greater internal

54

cohesion. Its common denominator was provided by the new, impatient nationalism of the masses. The growing strength of the movement had been demonstrated |in the recurring mass demonstrations and in the well-organized boycott movements. Following upon the wave of indignation set off by the Versailles bargainings, in 1922 and again two years later, there were widespread movements against Chinese Christians and against foreign missionary activities, leading to the demand that foreigners at the head of Christian educational institutions be replaced by Chinese. Then, in 1925, a powerful and violent wave of agitation spread to all the major ports directed at the 'unequal treaties' and against the British in particular. This led to violent clashes with British troops in both Shanghai and in Canton and culminated in a surprisingly effective boycott of British goods as well as in the blockade of Hong Kong. Rather than move her gunboats up the river, as used to be done in earlier years, Britain, in fact, had been participating in a conference in Peking devoted to the restoration of China's tariff autonomy.

Visibly, the pressure was growing to obtain the abolition of the special position enjoyed by foreigners in China. The revolution, so hesitant in the years following 1911, was gaining momentum. Yet before the revolutionary movement could attempt both the abolition of foreign privileges and the re-unification of the country, it had to acquire a still wider mass base. Two indispensable preliminaries remained. First, China's intellectuals had to complete their definition and interpretation of the revolution's ideals. Secondly, political and military organization was needed, able to convey the revolution's ideals to the masses and to provide the discipline required to bring unity to the country.

The Intellectuals

WHAT HAD BEEN MERE INTELLECTUAL PROBINGS before and after 1911, was now developing into a more systematic effort to analyse and to interpret the causes of China's weakness and to envisage its remedies. Moreover, if the intellectual unrest that had accompanied the Double Tenth had been practically confined to the coastal areas, the new effort was now reaching the interior and was even beginning to capture venerable seats of learning.

The 'New Tide' The *New Tide*, as this movement came to be known, began to influence every aspect of Chinese thinking. Its shock-troops came from the ranks of the fast growing number of students who—either in western-type schools in China or, even more often, abroad—had come in contact with new ideas. They had brought back with them a variety of convictions ranging from Communism to admiration for American Liberalism. Due perhaps to their Confucian background, they tended to associate themselves with particular schools of thought centred, as a rule, around a personality of learning and prestige. The resulting interplay of ideas had provided a particularly fertile soil for the theses propagated by the chief exponents of the *New Tide*.

Their principal platform became the National Peking University itself. Founded in 1898, it was revitalized in 1917 when Tsai Yuan-pei, a liberal scholar educated in Germany, was appointed as its Chancellor. Tsai, a great advocate of academic freedom, later invited Chen Tu-hsiu, perhaps the most revolutionary thinker in China at the time, to become Dean of the College of Letters of Peking University. He was enthusiastically supported by the younger generation of scholars, the most notable among whom was perhaps Dr Hu Shih. It was under the guidance of these two men that China's great movement for intellectual freedom had grown to historic proportions.

Chen Tu-hsiu Chen Tu-hsiu, though relatively little known in the West, was one of the intellectual architects of the new China. At the

56

beginning he published his views in *La Jeunesse*, a monthly review which he had edited since 1915 and which had a surprisingly wide circulation. In his articles he had repeatedly analysed the causes of China's ineffectiveness since 1911. For him, the 'neutral attitude of the people' was the root-cause and so he asked for greater dynamism and for wider participation. 'Whether in politics, scholarship, morality or literature'—he wrote later on—'the Western method and the Chinese method are two absolutely different things and can in no way be compromised or reconciled . . . if we decide to reform, then we must adopt the new Western method in all things and need not confine the issue by such nonsense as "national heritage" or "special circumstances". . . .'

Such language of course was anathema for the traditionalists. The two views were radically opposed and, inevitably, Chen Tu-hsiu had to carry his offensive against Confucianism itself. In a series of articles in *La Jeunesse* he attacked the Confucian heritage. In his view it stood for the complete denial of human rights. Its prescriptions—the doctrine of five relationships—could not be modified so as to suit modern conditions and so, according to him, were merely the ideological foundation of despotism.

That the principal spokesman of such uncompromising attacks on venerable traditions came to occupy one of the most respected posts in China's educational hierarchy, was already symptomatic of the rapidly changing intellectual climate. Nor was he without associates of comparable weight. Most notable among them was Dr Hu Shih, a man of great erudition and hailing from a family with scholarly traditions. Following his studies of philosophy at American universities, he returned to China and won a wide following among the young.

His name became primarily associated with China's literary revolution, both in its figurative and literary sense. His first contribution to the *New Tide* movement was in the form of a manifesto, published in 1917, calling for the generalization of popular language capable to bridge the gap between the *élite* and the people. This, the *pai hua*, the most widely spoken form

Literary reform

of the vernacular, was to replace the classical written language which in its spoken form had grown almost unintelligible even among the *literati*. *Pai hua*, or the spoken style, then, was to provide a mode of expression accessible to all but the illiterates. Hu Shih summed up his programme of literary reform in eight characteristic points: 'Avoid classical allusions; discard parallel construction of sentences; discard time-worn literary phrases and do not avoid popular speech. Emphasize grammatical construction; do not use sickly expressions when you are not sick; do not imitate the ancients. In short, write naturally in a language which can be understood.'

To appreciate fully the importance of Hu Shih's initiative it is well to remember that probably ninety per cent of China's population at the time was illiterate, and that among the remaining one-tenth the tiny minority of scholars had been expressing their ideas in a highly formalized, classical written language which had remained inaccessible even to the literate minority. Chen Tu-hsiu's enthusiastic support of Hu Shih's plea gave the *New Tide* movement an additional stimulant in helping the emancipation of language from its traditional shackles. In a sense it represented a victory for western liberal ideas as it helped to deprive the scholar-bureaucrats of their most effective instrument of superiority. It was perhaps the most far-reaching step in the preparation of mass participation in the country's political, cultural and even administrative activities.

A living language

The *pai hua*, or 'national speech', was spread by the schools. It became the language of reviews, newspapers and books of all sorts—from critical essays and novels to numerous translations. Within the context of the general movement for intellectual freedom and for the modernization of every aspect of Chinese life, the reform of language was a decisive component of the *Renaissance* or the *New Tide*. Fast growing numbers of people were coming into contact with new ideas. The critical methods of western thought were gaining new adherents. And the new spirit of inquiry and the adventure of intellectual discovery were perceptibly corroding old patterns and were making way for something entirely new in Chinese experience.

The Intellectuals

Lecturing in Chicago in 1933, Dr Hu Shih described the period in terms worth quoting: 'Three prominent features in [the Renaissance] movement reminded [the students] of the European Renaissance. First, it was a conscious movement to promote a new literature in the living language of the people to take the place of the classical literature of old. Second, it was a movement of conscious protest against many of the ideas and institutions in the traditional culture, and of conscious emancipation of the individual man and woman from the bondage of the forces of tradition. It was a movement of reason versus tradition, freedom versus authority, and glorification of life and human values versus their suppression. And lastly, strange enough, this new movement was led by men who knew their cultural heritage and tried to study it with new methodology of modern historical criticism and research. In all these directions the new movement which began in 1917 . . . was capturing the imagination and sympathy of the youth of the nation as something which promised and pointed to the new birth of an old people and an old civilization. . . .'

And Dr Hu continued: '. . . The conscious element in this movement is the result of long contact with the people and civilization of the West. It is only through contact and comparison that the relative value or worthlessness of the various cultural elements can be clearly and critically seen and understood. . . . Without the benefit of an intimate contact with the civilization of the West, there could not be the Chinese Renaissance. . . .'

All this of course did not fail to provoke vigorous opposition. It came from a variety of directions. There were the traditional scholars who were scandalized by the attacks on Confucianism. Cautious reformers, impressed by the West's irreconcilable contradictions—as expressed in the World War —called for synthesis and for selective adoption only. Others again, and in fast growing numbers, argued under the impact of the Russian Revolution. To them, the *New Tide*—however helpful in weakening the hold of Confucianism and in furthering the literary revolution—failed to offer a new social strategy.

Ideological conflict

The Chinese Revolution

The western liberalism it stood for appeared ineffective in face of China's chronic chaos. In fact, the doctrinal fall-out of Lenin's anti-liberal revolution descended on a China already disillusioned with the West's war and its attitude at the Versailles Conference, and even with a democracy apparently unable to translate its theories into institutions capable of offering stability to China.

Only a few years after the October Revolution, then, China's intellectuals were already separated on the two sides of the ideological barricades. By its very success perhaps the *New Tide* disguised its radical advance guard which was beginning to turn away from its original, liberal ideas. The greater the movement's influence became, the less it was able to catch up with the growing radicalism of the masses whom it had inspired. Ironically, one of the original founders of the Chinese Communist Party was none other than Chen Tu-hsiu, the very leader of the *New Tide* who had stood for unconditional westernization.

But intellectual cleavage merely foreshadowed an even graver divorce. It was to come among those who were destined to give a strategy and social content to the unifying political action for which the country had been waiting for so long.

The Kuomintang

IF THE RÉGIME OF YUAN SHIH-KAI had symbolized the revival of rule by military men around whom rallied the landlords and scholars, the liberal and republican protest came chiefly from the more radical South. The organizational expression of that republicanism was the Kuomintang, or the Nationalist Party.

Its origins go back to 1905 when, among Chinese students in Tokyo, Sun Yat-sen organized a revolutionary society, called the Tung Meng Hui. It stood for the overthrow of the Manchus, for the recovery of China for the Chinese, and for the establishment of a Republic strong enough to nationalize the land and to realize a series of other social reforms. Various clandestine revolutionary groupings within China had been in contact with Tung Meng Hui and looked to it for moral support. Thanks to Sun Yat-sen's influence in Chinese communities abroad, to their financial aid, and to his own organizational activities, the scattered groups gradually acquired the shape of a great political party. Already it was dominant in the Nanking Provisional Assembly. Then, during the war-lord period, it provided the base to the Canton régime which, in April 1921, elected Dr Sun as its first President. From that time onward right up to his death, his name and the fortunes of the Kuomintang had been indissolubly linked.

But the Party was not immune from the curse of Chinese politics of the time and was beset with petty factionalism. This was barely surprising if one considers that the Kuomintang was a heterogeneous body which embraced groups and classes with conflicting views of the future. Both big landlords and the scholar-bureaucrats were well represented within its ranks. Most of its leaders came from the rural gentry. The radical intellectuals in it were but a tiny and rather ineffective minority. The vague republicanism which was its binding cement appeared inadequate either to define the Party's programme or

A vague
Republicanism

to ensure its cohesion. In fact, Dr Sun himself repeatedly fell victim to intrigues for power within the Kuomintang. He was only the more vulnerable as the western powers had practically ignored him. He obtained from them no support, and they failed to recognize in the Kuomintang the political force it was to become. Thus, unaided, determined to persuade rather than to coerce, and in any case without the means to discipline the recalcitrants, Sun Yat-sen could never provide his Party with the power and the organization it would have needed to make his revolutionary political objectives triumph. When, on 12 March 1925, an incurable disease removed him from the Chinese political scene, he could not yet see any of the real results of his long and devoted work.

Yet some of the most significant decisions preparing the Kuomintang's success had been taken by Dr Sun long before his death. Their history provides the most controversial aspect of his otherwise single-minded and life-long patriotic activities.

Sun Yat-sen turns to Russia

Bitterly disappointed first by the support the western powers had given to Yuan Shih-kai, and impressed later on by both the anti-imperialist propaganda and the organization of the Russian Communists, Sun Yat-sen had become more and more convinced that strong executive power—resting on discipline and organization—were indispensable to translate ideals into reality. In order to provide the Kuomintang with such power, he gradually turned his face toward the Soviet Union, the only power at the time willing to help him. Moscow was far-sighted enough to recognize the revolutionary potentialities of the Kuomintang while the western powers were still offering their support to the war-lords. Though by no means seduced by the ideals of Communism, nevertheless Dr Sun grew convinced that China's revolution could not but profit from, what appeared to him, the USSR's disinterested aid. He needed both arms and civilian and military advisers. He obtained it all in January 1923 in the course of his decisive negotiations with Adolphe Joffe, sent to China by Stalin.

One of the interesting sequels to this agreement was Sun's decision to send to Russia one of his close collaborators,

Chiang Kai-shek. He was sent to study the situation in that country and the organization of the Red Army in particular. Following his return from Moscow, it was under his command that the Whampoa Military Academy was established at Canton. Intended to train the new Nationalist Army's officers and thus to forge the Kuomintang's major instrument of national unification, it was assured of Russian arms and instructors. Under Chiang Kai-shek, who was its military commander, the man who became its director of political education was Chou En-lai.

An even more significant decision was taken at the Kuomintang's first National Congress held in Canton in 1924. It permitted Communists to enter the ranks of the Kuomintang. In this way, while it was implicitly admitted that the Nationalists needed the Communists' organizational ability and techniques, the Kuomintang itself was thoroughly reorganized. Russian councillors, with Borodin foremost among them, were helping. And the new structure resembled in many ways the organization of the Russian Communist Party.

All this helped to give the Kuomintang a new shape and to prepare it for its coming great role. Sun Yat-sen, who had taken the decision, was the uncontested head of the new organization and his views its guiding principles.

In the eyes of westerners Sun Yat-sen was far from being a striking personality. He looked inconspicuous. His writings seemed but a collection of mediocre maxims devoid of originality. His views often seemed even obscure and the very terminology he had employed could barely be understood without placing them in their specifically Chinese context. Part of this vagueness was no doubt due to his endeavour not to accentuate the cleavage among China's intellectuals. He had to reassure those who feared the Treaty Powers' intervention in an effort to prevent Soviet aid reaching China. On the other hand, he had to convince others who, thinking of past experience, could not believe that no economic or political price was being paid for Russian assistance. As a result, his views on Socialism and Communism were probably intention-

A coherent philosophy

ally couched in elusive terms. His main concern was to emphasize points of agreement rather than to alienate waverers.

Nevertheless he was the first leader in modern Chinese history to offer a coherent philosophy to a society manifestly drifting and uncertain about its own values. However vaguely, he outlined a political strategy and defined its social content. For the first time the way to attain unity and independence was presented not in the form of abstract principles but in more or less practical terms. And for all these reasons Dr Sun's intellectual influence on his contemporaries was immense.

Dr Sun's three principles

After a lifetime of political activity, the synthesis of his views was given in a long series of lectures in Canton. Originally an admirer of western liberalism, by then Sun was disillusioned with parliamentary democracy as a practical ideal for China's immediate future. Following the October Revolution two more anti-liberal revolutions had occurred, in Kemalist Turkey and Fascist Italy, to strengthen his conviction. Though his economic ideas remained of a liberal and *bourgeois* nature, China's persistent disunity provoked his admiration for the strong, centralized and disciplined one-party State. His Canton lectures—interrupted by the disease that finally caused his death—were later edited in their present form and became known as the *San Min Chu I*, or Three People's Principles.

According to the translation prepared by Dr Sun's son, the Three Principles embrace National Democracy, Political Democracy, and Economic Democracy. The first stood for People's Nationalism—implying national unity and liberation from foreign control. The second, for Government by the People, to be attained in three stages. The third, for People's Livelihood, approximating to Socialism and including two highly important principles. One of them was the Land for the Tiller, and the second, the greater participation of the State in industrialization at the expense of the role of private capital. Traditional Chinese institutions and thinking were thus mixed with the experiences of both the liberal West and of the Soviet Union. The initial struggle against the war-lords apart, the principal socio-economic themes throughout his lectures had been evolutionary land-reform and the taming of private capital. All the time, however, Sun had emphasized his opposition to coercion and called for change through persuasion.

Sun Yat-sen proposed to attain the democracy thus defined in three stages. It was to begin with a period of purely military government. This was to yield to a phase of political tutelage under the party and amounting in practice to a period of apprenticeship in self-government. Only after the attainment of political consciousness by the masses would follow the third and final phase of a constitutional Republic with a popularly elected Parliament.

A humanitarian and an idealist, Sun had remained strangely unfamiliar with the power dynamics of daily politics. How the actual transition from one phase to the next was to be achieved, or how opposition to such gradual liberalization was to be overcome, he did not say. Though his *rapprochement* with Moscow might be interpreted as a desire to put teeth into the Kuomintang, how this programme could be implemented in daily practice remained unanswered till his death. So, inevitably, his followers inherited the difficult problem of how to put real executive power behind the political and social intentions contained in Sun's blue-print.

Blueprint without a plan

In reality, once the Nationalist Army was beginning to take shape and reunification was becoming a practical possibility, it was soon clear that the wielders of that new power, rather than realizing the ideals of the People's Livelihood, were fast slipping back toward alliance with the forces of the defunct old order.

Did he perhaps foresee what was to come? In any case, it was not the least of the ambiguities of Sun Yat-sen's life that from a missionary education and from admiration for western liberal institutions, he travelled far enough to end up with a comparable enthusiasm for the Soviet Union.

'. . . I hope that [the Kuomintang] will co-operate with you in the accomplishment of its historic task of the liberation of China and of the other countries under the imperialists' yoke'— he said in his last letter written on his death-bed, addressed to the Central Executive Committee of the Soviet Union. '. . . Taking leave of you, dear comrades,' he continued, 'I want to express the hope that the day will soon come when the USSR will become a friend and ally of a mighty, free China and that in the great struggle for the liberation of oppressed peoples of the world both those allies will go forward to victory hand in hand. . . .' And his disillusion with Chinese liberalism was soon confirmed by the events which were to follow his death.

But by the time the Kuomintang began to distort and to dilute the *San Min Chu I*, already there existed a rival political party which relied on powerful organizational techniques and was determined to give the revolution a much more radical content.

The Communists

THE REVOLUTIONARY PRESTIGE and propaganda emanating from Moscow, as much as the manifest inapplicability of the western parliamentary method to Chinese conditions, were natural stimulants to swell the number of Chinese intellectuals turning to the Marxist prescription.

In the big cities every 'ism' borrowed from the West had found its enthusiastic clan of followers. The visits, in 1919 and 1920, of John Dewey and of Bertrand Russell, also helped to stimulate the intellectual ferment. But the real raw material of Chinese Communism was the younger leaders of the *New Tide* itself. In practice, even more than Marx's theories, it was rather the economic and social example of the Soviet Union that helped to seduce them. Chen Tu-hsiu himself did not begin to study seriously Marx's writings until well after the October Revolution. Mao Tse-tung, assistant librarian at Peking University and strongly influenced by Li Ta-chao, dates his conversion to 1920 only.

It was in the spring of 1918 that a group of students, led by some of their Professors at Peking University, had turned to the systematic study of Marxism. In another two years Chen Tu-hsiu, together with Li Ta-chao, Dean of the Faculty of History, had grown finally disillusioned with their radical liberalism and become committed to Marxism-Leninism. Both had considerable influence over their students and, in collaboration with like-minded intellectuals, they began to organize Marxist study groups. It was under the guidance of Gregory Voitinsky, a Comintern agent in China, that these scattered groups were welded together so as to form the nucleus of the future Chinese Communist Party.

By the summer of 1921 the stage was set for its first Congress. It was held in secrecy, beginning on July 1, in a girls' school in the French Concession of Shanghai. Its deliberations having been disturbed by the police, the participants had fled to

The first Congress

67

Chekiang province in the South, where, at Shaohsing, they concluded their business in a boat on a lake.

First Chairman of the Party was Chen Tu-hsiu and one of the twelve delegates present was Mao Tse-tung. Though they were soon reinforced by various people returning from the West where they had studied or had organized Marxist groups among expatriate Chinese, and though they found sympathizers within China, at that stage the Chinese Communist Party had little influence and was barely more than a tiny band of enthusiastic young men united in their Communist faith. The twelve delegates present at the first Congress represented no more than fifty members. At the time of the second Congress held a year later, membership was still not higher than 123, composed mainly of intellectuals.

But progress was fairly rapid. Chen attended the fourth Congress of the Comintern in Moscow in November 1922. Afterwards, advised from outside and full of its sense of mission, the Chinese Communist Party began to turn its attention to the emerging proletariat in the towns. The main task the Party set itself was the organization of a labour federation. Industrial labour was ready to welcome such developments and the Party's influence had grown rapidly in the new unions, especially among railroad workers. Yet the Party was still too little known and had too little experience to justify its faith in a Bolshevik type of revolution in China. It seemed more than doubtful whether that stage could be reached at all without first passing through a *bourgeois* revolution as its indispensable preliminary. Such doubts were powerfully reinforced when, on 7 February 1923, the strike of the workers of the Peking–Hankow railway was suppressed in a veritable bloodbath. The demoralizing effect of this incident on the Chinese labour movement was very great. It could not fail to strengthen the case of the gradualists.

So, the temptation to bring about a wide revolutionary front—embracing workers, peasants and middle-class elements —had become much greater. Nor did Moscow have any illusions about the immediate prospects of China's Communists. For the Comintern, the Kuomintang was the rising revolutionary force and it was on its shoulders that Chinese Communism was eventually to ride to greater influence.

The first task of the Communists, then, was to penetrate the Kuomintang. Their well-known qualities helped bring off the deal. These were discipline, organizing ability, and a technique of raising the masses in support of the Nationalists' revolutionary aims. As the Kuomintang were sadly in need of precisely these qualities, Sun Yat-sen and the Nationalists were ready to meet half way both the Chinese Communists and the Soviet agents and instructors.

Penetrating the Kuomintang

Neglected by the western powers, Sun Yat-sen needed foreign aid. The Kuomintang needed the Communists to help stiffen its organization. But this very stiffening, brought about with Communist help, tended also to frustrate the Communists' basic aim, namely to penetrate and finally to master the Kuomintang. The Comintern thus helped to create a party beyond its control. But that wasn't all.

Both within the Kuomintang and inside the Communist Party there had been vocal opposition to their collaboration. The right wing of the Kuomintang, composed mainly of land-owning interests and relying on the hopes and on the backing of the nascent middle-classes in the coastal towns, had been apprehensive of the Communists' growing influence. Nor were some of the Communists less hesitant. Chen Tu-hsiu himself strongly criticized both the vagueness of Sun Yat-sen's doctrine and the looseness of the Kuomintang's organization. He believed that the Kuomintang should be left to carry out alone its '*bourgeois* revolution' and that the Communists ought to wait, as a separate entity, ready for the direction of the next, fully Communist stage.

Such and similar 'deviationism' in the Chinese Communist Party, however, merely mirrored comparable differences of opinion on the policy towards China existing in Moscow's leading circles. For Stalin, the northern war-lords were mere allies of the western powers and so, at that stage at any rate, their defeat—if need be through joint Kuomintang-

69

The Chinese Revolution

Communist action—was more urgent than the eventual triumph of the Communists over the Kuomintang. Trotsky, together with some other Russian leaders, disagreed. What policy to adopt toward China was, at the time, one of the chief bones of contention between the rival factions in the Kremlin.

But Stalin's views prevailed and the Chinese Communist Party—following Moscow's lead—opted for co-operation with the Kuomintang.

The Sun–Joffe declaration

The famous Sun–Joffe declaration in January 1923—the result of long negotiations in Japan—formally announced the coming collaboration between the two parties. The following year the Kuomintang authorized the entry of Communists into its organization 'as individuals'. It admitted that they might maintain their original allegiance to the Communist Party which might maintain its separate existence. This way co-operation was beginning to take on practical forms. Some prominent Communists, like Li Ta-chao and Mao Tse-tung, had been admitted to important functions within the Kuomintang organization. Michael Borodin, who had rendered similar services to Mustapha Kemal in Turkey, had come to Canton as the Comintern's adviser and he had been accompanied by a group of civil and military specialists to aid in the reorganization of the structure of the Kuomintang.

During 1924 and 1925 both parties had been making progress. Russian and Chinese Communists both helped to turn the Kuomintang into a disciplined organization and also to free it of its manifestly inapplicable liberal aspirations. In the meantime the new revolutionary army, by now led by officers trained at the Whampoa Military Academy, eliminated 'local war-lords' and became a firm support of the Canton Government. Simultaneously, the Communists not merely occupied some of the key posts but also reinforced their own organization and influence with the urban working classes. Under their leadership the latent anti-foreign and anti-imperialist forces had been mobilized behind strikes and demonstrations.

In Shanghai in 1925, and in Canton later on in the same year, they had occasion to show their force. Between 1922 and 1927 membership of the Party had grown from 300 to nearly 60,000. During the same period the number of workers organized in trade unions had passed from just over 200,000 to over three million. Though much slower, progress had also been made among the peasants, grouped in increasing numbers into large peasant organizations.

Whatever misgivings these developments may have provoked in the Kuomintang ranks, collaboration between the two parties remained more or less normal while Sun Yat-sen was the unchallenged leader. On 20 March 1926, profiting by an alleged Communist plot, Chiang Kai-shek, the successor of Dr Sun, and identified with the more conservative elements within the Party, seized effective power, dissolved the Hong Kong strike-committee, and eliminated several Communists from the higher positions they had occupied in the Kuomintang hierarchy. Continued co-operation was evidently under heavy strain.

The Alliance under strain

But before the antagonism so accentuated by Chiang's *coup d'état* could finally compromise the chances of further collaboration, and still following Moscow's directives, the Communists decided to maintain the alliance. Their main reason for doing so was that the day of action, in preparation for which they had joined the Kuomintang, was finally approaching.

By 1926 the nationalist armies were ready to move northward and so to begin the reunification of the country.

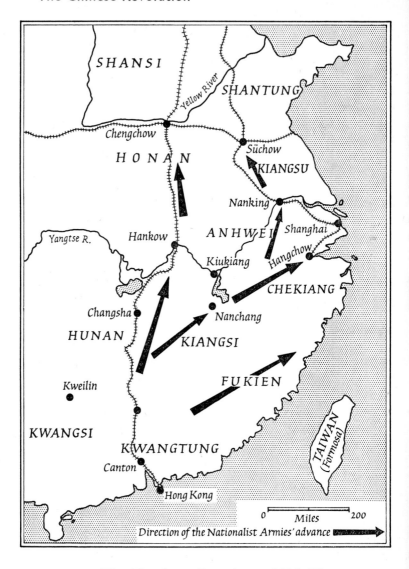

The Northern Expedition 1926–27

Cooperation and Showdown

By JULY 1926 the combined Kuomintang-Communist forces were ready for action. Starting out from the South, five armies spread out toward the North and East, in the direction of Hankow and Nanchang. Very soon it became clear that their campaign would bring the Nationalist Government to power on a wave of popular enthusiasm.

By this time the Kuomintang armies were by far the best equipped and the most modern among the various armed forces existing in China. Most of the troops had been trained by competent officers who themselves had been taught by Russian instructors. What was even more new, political agitators were both preceding and accompanying the marching columns. The armies could rely on a propaganda machine which prepared peasant support in the regions where they arrived, as well as on the enthusiastic co-operation of at least the young in the cities which were to be occupied.

The military governments which had been ruling the provinces had been more tyrannical and even more corrupt than had been the Manchu administration during its days of final decay. Thus the nationalist armies marched across provinces sick of long years of exactions, of insecurity and banditism and, in most cases, ready to welcome the liberators without a fight. As a matter of fact, in a number of regions the nationalist advance had been helped by popular risings forcing the warlords either to compromise or to withdraw. This way, though not entirely without some hard fighting, the advance was rapid. The city of Changsha fell by July 12. Wuhan, the great urban conglomeration on the two banks of the Yangtze, was liberated in October–November. Nanchang was taken by the end of October.

A liberation army

With most of the South and of Central China by then under the nationalists' control, their government, accompanied by Borodin, the Comintern adviser, moved forward from Canton

73

to Hankow, one of the three cities composing Wuhan. This, the so-called Wuhan Government, was dominated by the Kuomintang's left wing, by the Communists and by some of their sympathizers. Yet the decision to move north to Hankow was taken against Chiang Kai-shek's wish. His plan was to establish the new Government in Nanchang, free of the radical influences of the great Yangtze cities.

Hostility to foreign concessions

With the national liberation movement reaching the Yangtze valley and with the inevitable contact between the revolutionary armies and the foreign concessions, a number of delicate problems were bound to arise; problems which Chiang and the right wing of the Kuomintang would have preferred to face only later on. In the intensely anti-foreign and anti-capitalist atmosphere of Hankow, the political orientation of the Wuhan Government was bound to shift further to the left. Already some of its Ministers were Communists. And Communist influence in a number of fields was by then acquiring menacing proportions.

Inevitably conflicts developed and they soon put a heavy strain on Kuomintang-Communist collaboration. Demonstrators manipulated by pro-Communist and anti-imperialist agitators seized the British concessions in Hankow and Kiukiang and only the withdrawal of the British marines prevented serious bloodshed. Later on, in March 1927, pro-Communist elements took possession of Nanking. Simultaneously, large-scale strikes were organized in a number of towns and the anti-capitalist and anti-landlord forces seemed to be gaining the upper hand within the Kuomintang-Communist alliance.

All these developments, of course, could not fail to lead to violence. Some foreigners, including missionaries, were killed or manhandled. There was looting and the burning of some foreign property. In the meantime, though given much less attention in the world Press, foreign warships on China's rivers retaliated with the usual vindictiveness and with little regard for Chinese life, making probably many times more victims than had the outrages perpetrated by the Chinese demon-

74

strators. What was at stake was the sanctity of foreign privileges. If the basic aim of the nationalist armies was to unite China and to free her of imposed privileges, foreign interests were disposed to accept the nationalists' authority only in so far as it promised a stronger intermediary between the masses and themselves.

But the 'misunderstandings' thus emerging between the revolutionary forces and foreign interests, were secondary to the misunderstandings arising between the aims of the most influential of Kuomintang supporters and those of the masses just awakened to their new possibilities. This was particularly clear in the countryside where the nationalist armies had passed.

Demands for land reform

The landholding system, the power of the money-lenders allied to that of the landlords, together with the continuous fragmentation of holdings due to population growth, had maintained the Chinese countryside in a state of explosive expectation. The rural agitators preceding the nationalist armies discovered, not without amazement, that most of the peasants were only too ready to support their most revolutionary aims. In fact, very soon, the Communists, who were busy organizing in the villages, discovered that peasant radicalism would push far beyond what the imperatives of Communist-Kuomintang collaboration could accommodate. There appeared powerful agrarian movements calling for revolutionary changes. In several regions landlords were eliminated by savage methods and their land was confiscated and distributed among the landless peasants. Acting on instructions from party headquarters, the rural organizers attempted to limit the upheaval. They had to go even so far as to restore the confiscated land of officers serving in the Kuomintang armies. Nevertheless, the unexpected violence of the rural explosion could not fail to frighten the majority interests behind the Kuomintang, especially those which represented the big landlords and the rural gentry.

Anxious to avoid an open clash with the foreigners—which would have provided the Communists with an early opportunity to monopolize the leadership of the ensuing anti-foreign war—and menaced in its direct agrarian interests, the Kuomintang was rapidly driven to reconsider its precarious collaboration with the Communists.

When, in March 1927, the Wuhan Government decided to withdraw Chiang Kai-shek's special powers, given to him on the eve of the Northern Expedition, he knew that he had to act before it would be too late.

The emergence of Chiang Kai-shek

The very success of the campaign turned the limelight on its uncontested leader, on Generalissimo Chiang Kai-shek. His prestige had greatly increased and he emerged as a national hero. To that extent he grew less dependent on the Russian and Communist aid which had been indispensable to ensure the success of the march north. So, he was preparing to rid himself of the obligations arising from the alliance. Simultaneously, however, the territorial expansion of the nationalists' authority had opened up before the Communists an immense new field for the work of their rural agitators and organizers. If some Communists had been uneasy with the alliance right from the beginning, others began to believe that the moment had arrived to assert Communist supremacy at least over the left wing of the Kuomintang.

Moscow was clearly behind the latter. Though Stalin had no illusions about the reliability of Chiang as a political ally, he still believed that the best chance for the Chinese Communists to fortify their hold over the country, was within the Kuomintang. The resulting situation was far from comfortable for China's Communists. Constantly they had to moderate the very forces they had helped to create. That at least some of their leaders regarded such tactics as suicidal, is hardly surprising.

The Nanking rising

It was against such a background that the Communist inspired rising occurred in Nanking in March 1927. To forestall similar developments in the citadel of foreign interests and of the Chinese *bourgeoisie* itself, Chiang Kai-shek rushed to Shanghai. The real story of the fateful days while his troops approached the city and while he negotiated with the representatives of the financial interests having their headquarters in it, are not yet fully known.

The foreigners and the Chinese financial, industrial and merchant interests, through their Shanghai spokesmen, appeared to be ready to accept the Kuomintang, but only on condition that it rid itself of the Communists and of the influence of its own radicals. As for Chiang himself, to consolidate the areas already gained must have appeared to him more desirable than to pursue the Kuomintang's advance. By now this would have involved the risk of open clash with western and Japanese interests entrenched in the coastal and in the northern areas.

All these considerations no doubt greatly helped the progress of the secret negotiations which had been carried on between Chiang, the big banking interests of Shanghai, and between the secret societies in the latter's pay.

Their outcome was a bargain destined to change the course of China's revolution.

Chiang Kai-shek entered Shanghai on March 22. Barely three weeks later, on 12 April 1927, the people of that great metropolis woke to the sound of intermittent gun fire in the streets.

The Generalissimo was ready for the break. He decided to turn against the allies he had needed to make a success of the Northern Expedition. Leading Communists and leaders of trade unions and of workers' organizations were arrested and summarily executed. Shanghai's secret societies were helping to hunt down the underground workers' committees which had been prepared for the take-over of the city.

Chiang's coup d'état

In Shanghai, as in a number of other towns from Canton to Peking, there began the savage massacre of Communists and of their sympathizers. Public mass-executions continued for several days, often carried out with deliberate cruelty. Tens of thousands of individuals were either killed, disappeared, or were herded into prisons. A few prominent Communists managed to escape. Chou En-lai himself, captured in Shanghai and ordered to be shot, owed his life to the accident that the man in charge of his execution turned out to be one of his former pupils at the Whampoa Military Academy and let him escape. A few, like Mao Tse-tung, were away from the cities, hiding in the countryside. Numerous others, including Li Ta-chao, the co-founder of the party, were less lucky and lost their lives.

Next to them, the principal casualty of Chiang's *coup d'état* was the political heritage of Sun Yat-sen. No compromise could any longer contain the contradictions in the composition of the nationalist forces. Only three years after the death of Dr Sun, the uneasy ideological armistice was at its end. Unification, one of the principal aims of the nationalist revolution, being within sight, the Kuomintang machine needed no longer the ideological cement or the organizational abilities of the Communists. As for the political conceptions which Moscow had imposed on China's Communist Party, they were in ruins.

Kuomintang takes over

During the weeks following the April *coup*, the completeness of the break was soon revealed. The Wuhan Government broke off its relations with Chiang Kai-shek who, shortly after, installed his own Nationalist Government in Nanking. Even the alliance between the Kuomintang's left wing and the Communists began to disintegrate. Borodin fled the country. Some prominent Communists and their sympathizers—including the widow of Sun Yat-sen, the sister of the Generalissimo's wife—sought refuge in the Soviet Union. Moscow's continued hesitations only hastened the decline and caused it to be punctuated by desperate and suicidal risings. The left wing Wuhan remnant of the Kuomintang broke with the Communists in July. And to crown the defection of friends and allies, on 1 August 1927, part of the garrison of Nanchang (in Kiangsi) mutinied against their Communist generals, thus marking the definite end of all collaboration between Kuomintang and Communists. And while the Communists had become outlaws all over the country, the Kuomintang, established in its new capital at Nanking, obtained the western powers' recognition as the national government of all China.

At last the country seemed to emerge from decades of anarchy. Noting how weak and utterly beaten the Communists were, many observers concluded that the story of the Revolution itself was concluded. Others, more circumspect, sensed that what had happened had been only a process of simplification. In place of the long list of potential founders of dynasties, of parties, clans and war-lords, now there remained two main antagonists only. And though they appeared vastly unequal in strength, their contest was to provide the main theme of two more acts to come.

Part Three

Reunification and Advance

AFTER THE NANCHANG RISING the road seemed to be open to reconciliation between what remained of the Wuhan Government and Chiang's régime and so to end the war of reunification. But in reality things were less simple. Through the confusing and complex maze of negotiations, bargainings, intrigues and betrayals, unification made little progress during the months which followed the Shanghai show-down.

Chiang himself went into semi-voluntary exile in Japan. He returned a few months later only, in December 1927, once the chances of unity had somewhat improved. First he disciplined the opposing generals. Then he settled with the Powers the differences over the issues arising from the Nanking rising. After that, with his position reinforced, fighting and bargaining his way through, he continued to extend the authority of his government.

In June 1928 when the nationalist forces occupied Peking, the Kuomintang could claim that it had imposed a higher degree of unity on China than the country had known since the turn of the century. Its hold was firm in the Yangtze Valley and in some of the coastal provinces. Over the rest of the country it was often more apparent than real. In certain regions war-lords, commanding their own armies, were still supreme. Up to his death in 1928, Chang Tso-lin was in effective control of Manchuria and for another two years his son carried on a pro-Japanese policy, independent of Nanking's will. Some governors appointed by the Kuomintang became virtually independent. As for the border regions, even if Tibet was persuaded to recognize Nanking's sovereignty, the huge, north-western province of Sinkiang refused to treat with the Nationalist Government and was virtually under Russian protection.

All this being said, however, the formal reunification of most of China was practically accomplished by the summer of 1928.

The Chinese Revolution

In theory, at least, the military stage of the revolution was completed. In Sun Yat-sen's terms the period of political tutelage under a single party—expected to lead to constitutional government—was to begin. And the period of Kuomintang tutelage was to be devoted to two principal tasks.

Recovering full sovereignty

To begin with, the attempts to recover China's full sovereignty were to continue so as to give real meaning to the revolution's declared aim of national liberation. Secondly, it was the government's aim to strengthen and to modernize the country, to overcome its backwardness in education and technology, in order to speed its economic development.

The determination to free the country from the restrictions which had been imposed on its sovereignty, was one of the most dynamic ingredients of the ideal that backed the Northern Expedition. The international context merely helped to fire such passions. Asia was in the forefront of the global revolt against western domination and white men were its obvious targets. Inevitably, there were clashes with foreigners once the Kuomintang armies reached the Yangtze Valley and took cities with important and rich white minorities. Although after the break with the Communists the Kuomintang wished to improve its relations with foreigners, and to that extent its attitude became much more cautious, its basic aims were not modified. Indeed, the Kuomintang's later record ought not make one forget its achievements in its first years. Perhaps none of them was more significant than the progress it had made toward the gradual relinquishing of the foreigners' privileges in China.

Already by 1927 most of the powers had abandoned their claim to the unpaid portions of the Boxer indemnity. Their gesture clearly implied that they no longer wished to be identified with the vindictive punishment inflicted on the country at the beginning of the century.

Equally symptomatic of the changing atmosphere was the decision in January 1927 to restore to China the Mixed Court in Shanghai where, since 1911, Chinese had been tried by foreigners in their own country.

Another psychologically important move was the transfer of the capital from Peking to Nanking, in conformity with Sun Yat-sen's wish. Nanking, of course, was nearer to the country's seats of modern economic power. But the real significance of the transfer lay in the fact that the central government had moved away from the humiliating presence of alien troops protecting the diplomatic representatives of foreign powers. Nanking had neither Legation Quarters, foreign garrisons, nor the petrified souvenirs of a subservient imperial past.

A new capital

In the economic field, in 1928 the western powers agreed to the resumption of tariff autonomy by China. Their only condition was that no new privileges should be accorded to any one power at the expense of the others. Two years later Japan too gave her agreement. In February 1929 a new schedule of customs duties came into effect, this time fixed by China herself. Although the customs service was still in the hands of foreigners, from that date onward only Chinese were admitted to the staff and some were soon raised to the highest posts. Simultaneously, several powers—including Italy, Spain and Portugal—accepted for the first time that their nationals might have to pay taxes in China.

The far more difficult problem of extra-territorial powers was also taken up by the Nationalist Government. Those of Germany and of the Soviet Union had been surrendered already. Now China notified the other powers that upon expiry of their extra-territorial rights, new treaties would be negotiated and on a basis of complete equality and reciprocity. By 1928 nearly half the foreigners living in China had already lost their extra-territorial privileges. Those of the citizens of Great Britain, France, Japan and the United States, however, were not yet affected. Then, in December 1929 China announced that all extra-territorial rights would be terminated by New Year's Day 1930. Implementation of the threat, however, had to be postponed by two years. In between, Japan invaded Manchuria and action was indefinitely postponed.

An end to extra-territorial rights

During the same period the Nanking Government secured the surrender of the British concessions in Chinkiang, Kukiang,

Hankow and Amoy, while Chinese were admitted to the councils of the International Settlements in Shanghai. Still, three major issues remained outstanding: the complete abolition of extra-territoriality and of concession territories, Japan's privileges in the north of the country, and the utilization of the inland waterways by foreign vessels, including warships on the Yangtze. But by the time these could have been taken up, hostilities in Manchuria began. Facing Japan's aggression, the Kuomintang was obliged to adopt more conciliatory attitudes toward the West and China's claims were pressed no further.

But even so, four years after the Kuomintang's triumph much of the edifice of foreign privilege which had taken nearly a century to establish, was already dismantled. No foreign power felt inclined any longer to back up its demands with a show of naked force or to use it for the protection of its nationals. The only exception was Japan. And when she invaded Manchuria, the rapid progress the Kuomintang had been making in abolishing the foreigners' imposed rights, came to a temporary halt.

Forcing the retreat of foreign privileges from China was but one of the early successes of the Nationalist Government. Convalescing from decades of chaos and civil strife, China was advancing in several fields. Her point of departure had been so low that a little less disorder, a little more stability and only slightly improved organization were bound to yield impressive results.

New forms of government

The Nanking Government wished to build a modern apparatus of government. Its claim that it had become nationwide was not entirely without foundation. The organization was pyramidal, bearing the mark of the Soviet counsellors' influence. At the top, as in the Soviet Union, the party was controlling the government; theoretically through the National Congress, but in practice through the Kuomintang's Central Executive Committee. At the base, on the level of the local administrative unit, it was the executive committee formed of local party members that exercised the same control. As for the government itself, it had five main divisions, in conformity with Sun Yat-sen's ideas. Next to the executive, legislative and judicial branches, there were also the so-called examining and control divisions, symbols of the tutelage supposed to lead to fully-fledged democratic institutions later on. The five branches functioned under the Council of State, or cabinet, headed by the President, Chiang Kai-shek. In place of an ideology, there was the cult of Sun's memory. His portrait was in every office and class-room and silence was observed or the party song was sung in front of it as substitutes for the myth a totalitarian party needs. And the lip-service paid to the *San Min Chu I* tended to replace what ought to have been the programme of the new régime.

The interpretation of Dr Sun's Three People's Principles, however, became a highly selective performance. The vagueness of its language was a great help. Yet what was clearly its social content was conveniently ignored. The social composition of the Kuomintang, the personality of its leader, as much as the international context, exercised pressures which produced the compromise.

To begin with, the Nationalist Government followed up its break with the Communists with the severing of its diplomatic relations with the Soviet Union. This helped to reassure those at home who had been afraid that the revolution was getting out of hand. The urban interests, fast growing into a major political force, had to be considered. Chinese insurance and shipping companies, individual industrialists, bankers and merchants were beginning to represent pressure groups whose power was reinforced by the wealthier overseas Chinese whose remittances had helped to finance the revolution and were helping to cover China's unfavourable balance of trade. How far was the new government to represent their interests? In what form was it to recompense the aid the new capitalists had offered in Shanghai and elsewhere to help the Northern Expedition to triumph? Then, what political weight was to be given to the inland provinces where the landlords constituted the dominant class and where the Kuomintang organization itself was in the hands of the local gentry? Finally, what

Reconciling pressure groups

The Chinese Revolution

political role should be given to the Army whose recruits were sons of peasants dreaming of land reform, but most of whose officers came from land-owning families?

To reconcile views so radically opposed could, at best, only lead to an uneasy compromise. And uneasy it was. Yet in spite of it China was clearly forging ahead.

Opportunity and expansion

For the first time after long years of frustrating sterility, young Chinese had the sensation that unlimited opportunities were opening up before them. Those who had studied abroad or who obtained modern education in China, felt that at last they could apply their skills to the modernization of their country. Large projects were afoot in irrigation, in railway and road building, and in the planning of an industrial future. Hospitals were built, cotton was cultivated on newly recovered land, and large numbers of foreign experts were invited to help speed development. There was a visible increase in the number of automobiles and trucks on the roads. The movement of passengers and goods was on the increase and, proportionately, a new national consciousness was emerging from the new inter-provincial mobility. In the coastal cities, in particular, factories were put up for the manufacture of cotton textiles, for consumer goods, and for the production of simpler machines. A beginning was made even with heavy industry.

As a first consequence, imports of cotton yarn and textiles were in sharp decline. In contrast, machines were constituting a growing share of imports. Meanwhile, next to traditional exports like silk and tea, new ones appeared including even the products of the new cotton mills. As an index of the rural areas' thirst for progress, the quantity of kerosene used—principally for lighting in the villages—had about trebled during the first third of the century. Moreover, a fast growing proportion of exports and imports was carried in boats operated and owned by Chinese and their merchant and insurance companies were handling an increasing share of China's foreign trade. Though the country's dominant financial institutions were still foreign, Chinese-owned banks were beginning to claim their share of what used to be a foreign monopoly.

88

Encouraging as these developments had been, they were not free of some disquieting features. There was no general plan or co-ordination. Also imports of foodstuffs were on the increase. Although an overwhelmingly agrarian country, China was not coming nearer to feeding her population. Famines were still recurring. Notwithstanding the growing volume of exports, China's share in world trade was still insignificant and wholly disproportionate to her size. The country was still running a chronic deficit in its foreign trade. Other difficulties, less connected with the economic situation, concerned the administrative apparatus and even the political orientation of the Nationalist régime.

Lack of planning and direction

Once its initial drive was over, it became apparent that the administrative efficiency of the new régime was barely superior to that of its predecessors. Creeping inflation continued and the problem of currency stabilization was never seriously tackled. What was even more serious, the Kuomintang, right from the beginning, could never eliminate corruption. With the passage of time it had grown to alarming proportions and seemed bound to undermine the prestige of the government. Above all, the harsh authoritarianism of the Kuomintang prevented even moderate criticism of its policies and had driven underground the expression of discontent in any form. Long disillusioned in their hope of seeing a liberal government, or of enjoying even elementary civil liberties, most educated Chinese would have put up with the intolerance of the Nationalist Government had they felt that it was mitigated by serious intent to face China's basic problem: the desperate poverty of the countryside. Instead, more and more clearly, reform was blocked by the powerful landed interests within the Party and the already strong and privileged were growing still more powerful at the expense of the great majority.

If in its first years the Nationalist Government brought change and progress, by the early 'thirties its shortcomings had become painfully apparent. To change China would have been in any case a herculean task. Yet the Kuomintang seemed unable to offer remedies for any of the country's basic ills. A

A shadow of frustration

89

Shift to the Right

FOLLOWING ITS TRIUMPH, two courses of action were open to the Kuomintang.

It might have decided to give practical content to the economic and social promises implicit in *San Min Chu I*. This would have required a convincing effort to meet the basic needs of the peasant masses. An impartial administration, the promotion of the least privileged categories and, above all, a sweeping land reform would have been its major instruments. Such a programme would have gained the enthusiastic support of the majority of the population, of the young intellectuals dreaming of social justice, of the technicians and the specialists waiting for new opportunities, as well as of the enlightened and patriotic sections of the rising *bourgeoisie* aware of the need for wider internal markets to promote economic and industrial development. Such a wide programme of reform might have given the Kuomintang the broad popular support it would have needed to combat the propaganda of the Communists in the country and to prepare for the threat of aggression coming from outside.

Alternatively, the Kuomintang could attempt to build its authority on the unholy trinity of landlords, financiers and conservative scholar-officials; to profess loyalty to Dr Sun's principles while emptying them of their real content; to maintain its power by force of arms, repression and compromise; and to divert attention from basic issues by the manipulation of modern slogans unrelated to any real problems.

The Nationalist Government opted for the second course. It may be that the dilemma never really existed. Before 1927 already the grip of the landlords, the militarists and the traditionalist elements on the Kuomintang organization was very strong. After the break with the Communists it became decisive. Gradually, they moved up to occupy the highest posts in the party hierarchy. More and more, such elements, repre-

The fatal choice

senting the old order, personified the Kuomintang in its every-day contact with the masses. Occupying key-posts on every level, in the towns and in the countryside, they could effectively frustrate reform and commit the Kuomintang to uncompromising opposition to social change.

Whether it was the Kuomintang leadership that went farther than was necessary to cement alliances with the forces of the old society, or whether those forces have determined the party's course, may be a theoretical question only. What really mattered was the régime's performance in the eyes of the Chinese.

In practice, regional war-lords and semi-independent régimes kept on emerging from the maze of intrigues and bargains and the unification of the country seemed more and more nominal. Political, judicial and economic power in the countryside was in the hands of the land-owning class and its intermediaries. In matters most directly affecting the peasants—like the administration of their villages or the amount of taxes they had to pay—the Kuomintang could enforce neither efficiency nor justice. Principles were regularly sacrificed to serve private interests and the weight of Nanking's military power unfailingly came down on the side of established privileges. The very methods employed to enforce and to maintain the government's authority, however, helped to cut it off from popular sentiment. The peasants gave up all hope of seeing their grievances remedied by the authorities. The government ceased to hold out hope to the oppressed. In fact, the cancer of the Kuomintang was its growing indifference to the needs of the masses.

Evading the land problem

Nowhere perhaps had this divorce more tragic consequences than in the Nationalist régime's obstinate refusal to face the all-important land problem.

Growth of population, the declining individual share of cultivable land, its unequal distribution, high rents and still higher interest rates collected by the money-lenders, maintained the majority of peasants as prisoners of an infernal cycle. Barely above the subsistence level, without any margin of safety, drought or flood brought tragedy. Exorbitant rents and interest rates spread insecurity and that merely helped to drive interest rates and rents still higher. Yet after a bad harvest the farmer was driven to the money-lender, to place his land under mortgage and to accept such high interest rates that he would never finish paying off the loan and would ultimately lose his land.

All this, together with high taxation by local régimes, particularly in areas under war-lords, put the majority of farmers under intolerable pressure. That dangerous explosive forces were thus created, or that change was needed, was generally admitted. But how to proceed was less easy to decide. Some of the more far-sighted counsellors of the Kuomintang were urging the government to act. But political power was in the hands of the landlords who were often also the money-lenders. Even the most generous compensatory scheme would have been against their immediate interests. Yet in the early 1930s there was some hesitation in view of the urgency of the problem. At one stage a pilot scheme was envisaged in the province of Kiangsi to try out agrarian reform on a limited scale. In 1934 a group of experts of the League of Nations were invited to help draw up the detailed land reform programme. But this, as many other projects of a similar nature, never got beyond the stage of intentions.

Instead, the more convenient method was resorted to of passing apparently satisfactory legislation which was never seriously enforced. This way a law was passed ordering the lowering of farm rents to 37.5 per cent of the crop yield, and the abolition of sub-tenancy and the right of perpetual lease. It remained on paper. The landlords continued to collect rents going from a half to over two-thirds of the harvest. Interest rates were never controlled and there was no alternative cheap rural credit. Not infrequently, after payment of his rent, his interest rates and of his taxes, the cultivator was left with no more than a fifth, or perhaps even less, of the fruit of his labour.

Inaction and injustice

Evidently, injustice on such a monumental scale could not be lasting. But there was no philosophy or theory of reform to inspire change. Nationalism alone was not enough. And the power structure of the Nanking régime seemed such that manœuvring for advantages among its privileged groups diverted attention from even the most obviously urgent problems. The danger, of course, did not escape at least the more far-sighted of the Kuomintang functionaries. But they were usually far from the levers of power. Those in control of them were busy protecting clearly defined interests. And the man who presided over the Kuomintang's destinies was not merely too dependent on them but also lacked the political vision to comprehend the suicidal barrenness of such a course.

The character of Chiang Kai-shek

If, for the first quarter of the century, Sun Yat-sen's idealism served the revolution as its lighthouse, for the two decades following its triumph Chiang Kai-shek determined and charted its course. During those two decades his own character, the dominant forces of Chinese society, and international events were intertwined. To the misfortune of China all three proved to be inflexible.

Born in Chekiang province, Chiang came from the more modest layer of the landed gentry. Widowed, his mother had to work hard to secure him an education in the traditional Confucian spirit. But fairly young, Chiang decided for a military career. In China first, in Tokyo after, he completed his military studies. In Japan already he got associated with Sun's revolutionary activities and in 1911, back in Shanghai, he joined the republican army. During the hard years of the Canton Government he worked with Sun Yat-sen in the southern capital. After his mission in Russia and his direction of the Whampoa Military Academy, and following Dr Sun's death, he emerged as the Kuomintang's dominant personality. Once the Northern Expedition was about to be launched, he was the natural choice to be its commander-in-chief. In that role, at the age of forty, with the floodlights on him, he became China's man of destiny.

In the eyes of the foreign powers he was the potential strong man who would re-establish law and order and with whom a bargain might be struck. For the rising middle-classes he was the one man powerful enough to rid the Kuomintang of the dreaded infiltration of the Communists. Patriots expected him to unify their country. And the average Chinese hoped that he would bring progress, more justice and would restore the nation's damaged self-respect.

Chiang's positive qualities for military leadership were obvious. His austerity and physical courage were known. He was honest and uncompromising in his patriotism. He was both persevering in the pursuit of his ideals and commanding in his obstinacy. His qualities for political leadership, however, were less evident.

His education was patchy. His writings reveal a rather limited intellectual horizon. His deep-seated attachment to the hierarchical concepts of Confucianism made him totally insensitive to the interplay of social forces. Moreover, his puritanical attachment to the traditional order of things made him equate demand for structural change with betrayal of China's inherited grandeur. Gradually, the defence of his values became the protection of the existing social order.

Due perhaps to his modest origin, or simply by accident, Chiang Kai-shek's personal career unfailingly led him toward the summit of that existing social order, until he grew closely associated with its richest and most powerful representatives.

During his brief retirement in 1927, Chiang married as a second wife a daughter of James Soong, a banker and founder of one of the greatest fortunes in modern China. The Soong sisters were destined to play an important role in contemporary Chinese history. One of them was the wife of Sun Yat-sen. Another married H. H. Kung, a descendant of Confucius but also a banker and industrialist, who too was one of the richest men in the country. T. V. Soong, the brother of Mme Chiang and inheritor of the family fortune, was himself one of China's most influential financiers. Kung was a Protestant while the Soong family were Methodists. And Chiang himself was later given baptism into the Methodist faith.

Alliance with the new capitalism

T. V. Soong and H. H. Kung—both American educated— were to play decisive roles during the Kuomintang's rule as political and economic leaders in the government. Built, then,

The Chinese Revolution

as it were, on the common denominator of the Soong sisters, the political and economic leadership of the Kuomintang entered into a more than symbolic alliance with China's aggressive, modern capitalism. It was personified by the two dominant businessmen of the country, both brothers-in-law of the Generalissimo.

It is possible that such intimacy with the top layer of Chinese capitalism had helped to harden Chiang's hatred of Communism. But his opinions had already been formed. His ideas of propriety and his respect for tradition rendered him allergic to the Communists' fanatical dissent. He had returned from Russia with an intense dislike for their ideas and methods. If his admiration for Sun's nationalism made him acquiesce in the alliance with the Communists, he never considered it to be more than but temporary. Yet some basic contradictions in Chiang's character worked in the same direction.

Insensitivity and intolerance

Much as he was devoted to the national interest he was curiously insensitive to individual suffering, even when it was the suffering of his own troops and at the expense of their fighting morale. His overestimation of the importance of financial power as the expression of established order, went together with indifference to public opinion or to the need for reform and social change. Then, though conscious of presiding over a period of transition, he was unable to tolerate opposition. His hatred of Communism, the living and dynamic contradiction of all he stood for, grew into an obsession. And that obsession accompanied him like a shadow from Canton to the Shanghai massacres, and from his alliance with the bankers and industrialists right to the strategic conception of the wars he was to conduct.

From time to time it seemed as if Chiang Kai-shek had suddenly become conscious of some of the shortcomings of his régime. There were short-lived initiatives to correct some of the malpractices. In between, there had been some progress. Roads and schools were built. There were movements to promote literacy. Chinese enterprise was gaining ground in business and industry. Yet, simultaneously, already very rich men were amassing fabulous fortunes. The luxury of a small urban minority was setting it even more apart than before from the unremedied and abject poverty of the enormous majority. And corruption was growing to alarming proportions. Then, as, for example, in February 1934, a broader attempt would be made to change the rapidly deteriorating social climate. This, the New Life Movement, was a somewhat pathetic experiment to impose the Generalissimo's personal, puritanical ideals on a society increasingly disillusioned by the practices and the performance of the government over which he himself presided. It sought to encourage the revival of traditional virtues like devotion to public welfare, honesty, courtesy or personal cleanliness. But like other initiatives of the government, it failed to move the masses. Like the others, it lacked popular roots.

In what direction the Kuomintang might have developed if given more time, or whether it could still have extricated itself from the grip of naked reaction and change its course, it is impossible to tell. As it happened, time was running short. Internal and external threats were to interrupt and to change the Kuomintang's course. Barely four years after the Northern Expedition, China found herself in limited hostilities with Japan. In another six years they were to broaden into all-out war. Meanwhile, from 1932 onwards, the Communists, believed to have been annihilated as a political force, emerged as a graver threat to the government's authority than they had ever been before.

And by the time the Kuomintang had to face the double challenge, it was already doubtful whether it could command the popular support it needed.

Time runs out

97

Return of the Communists

AFTER ITS ROUT, the unity of what survived of the Chinese Communist Party was seriously affected. Like scattered parts of a mechanism smashed up by a hammer, each continued to function independently and without an overall political strategy. There existed, of course, a Central Committee in Shanghai as well as other symbols of party discipline. But in practice there was scarcely any uniformity. Rather it seemed as if each group was trying to draw its own lessons from the débâcle of 1927.

The ensuing process of selection and elimination was to last for about three years.

Yet this search for a new strategy coincided with the most critical period of the struggle for power between Stalin and Trotsky. China policy remained one of the main subjects of the great debate in the Kremlin. Stalin's and thus the Comintern's views were strongly influenced by the desire to vindicate the Soviet leader's earlier decisions and so to prove that Trotsky's diagnosis of the Chinese situation had been incorrect. This way, just when a totally new approach would have been needed, Moscow offered but ambiguous compromises so as to justify the claim that there was continuity in Stalin's China policy.

Three considerations were uppermost behind the chaotic decisions and compromises of that transitory period. As it was no longer possible to hope that the Kuomintang machine could be captured from the inside, the Comintern acquiesced, though only vaguely, in the creation in China of a separate, Communist military force. This marked the emergence of the Chinese Red Army. As for the main pattern of the revolutionary strategy of Chinese Communism, it was still to be modelled on Russian experience and was to be spearheaded by the city proletariat. To confirm this, and notwithstanding the highly unfavourable situation, a series of hopeless urban risings

followed. Simultaneously, however, the revolutionary radicalism of the peasantry could no longer be denied and had to be
allowed expression in the form of embryonic rural Soviets.

In this way, after the Nanchang rising in August 1927,   A Red Army
scattered partisan groups were arising in different parts of the
country. Under generals committed to the Communist cause,
they were gradually organized into small Red Armies. But, at
the same time, the urban risings continued. Thus the city of
Swatow was taken in September and was occupied for a week.
Two months later an insurrection was organized in Canton
which held the city between December 11 and 14. But from
Nanchang to Canton, all these desperate attempts to prove the
existence of the 'proletarian base' had been crushed and ended
in bloody repression. They merely helped to confirm growing
sentiment among Chinese workers that they were being sacrificed in the pursuit of unrealistic policies.

In the meantime there were also insurrectionary attempts in
the countryside. This way, Mao Tse-tung had been sent to his
native Hunan province to organize peasant disturbances there.
This in the hope that they might provide the spark for the
flame that would engulf all China and would then be guided by
the proletariat of the big cities. The result, the so-called Autumn
Harvest Rising in September 1927, failed to spread and was
finally extinguished by the usual repression. Following this,
Mao Tse-tung and the remnants of his forces withdrew to the
mountainous border area between Kiangsi and Fukien provinces. There, in Chingkanshan, he began to organize so as to
consolidate his position. Nor was he the only one to do so.
In November of the same year, Peng Pai, another rural
organizer, managed to form a peasant militia and to establish
the first Chinese Soviet Government in the sparsely populated
Haifeng and Lufeng areas not far away. In fact, several small,
rural Soviets were springing up around the same region, thus
justifying references to the 'Kiangsi soviets'.

Meanwhile Moscow's modifications of tactics as much as   Moscow
the rivalry of theses within the Chinese party itself, caused a   calls the tune
series of changes in leadership. First Chen Tu-hsiu was

removed, blamed for the misfortunes of the past. Branded as a 'right-opportunist' first, later on he was expelled from the party. Arrested by the Kuomintang, finally he died in liberty in 1942 though by then he had almost faded into obscurity. Under his successors new lines and new compromises were worked out, each attempting to harmonize Chinese reality with doctrinal rigidity. A fast shrinking following in the cities, and growing evidence of success among the rural masses, was incompatible with the dogma of leadership by the urban workers. Yet as a last desperate gesture to prove the supremacy of the urban proletarian base, the attempt was made to occupy a large industrial city. Thus Changsha, a town not far from the areas where Soviets had already been established in the country-side, was attacked in July 1930. But after a few days the insurgents were driven out of the city and their defeat, like the failure of the Canton Commune three years earlier, caused profound disillusionment in the Communist ranks. It was to be the last of the spectacular strokes.

'Playing with uprisings' was to be abandoned. And the complete re-thinking and re-orientation of strategy could finally be postponed no longer.

New factors   In the course of these three confused years, however, three decisively new factors emerged, destined to change the course of the Chinese Communist movement. It had become clear beyond doubt that the proletarian wing of the party was too weak and lacked sufficient popular support to make any real progress. Simultaneously, through the scattered rural Soviets, Chinese Communism was beginning to acquire a modest territorial base. Finally, in the form of small Red Armies, obliged to adopt guerilla tactics, Chinese Communism was beginning to forge its own arm of conquest.

Undoubtedly such a shift in the movement's political centre of gravity to the rural areas, was regarded with distrust by the Comintern. There is evidence that everything in Moscow's power was done to hinder such developments and that the principal engineers of that shift—with Mao Tse-tung foremost among them—had not merely been censured by the party leadership in Shanghai, but that they for a time even acted independently and against party directives.

Yet the trend could not be arrested. The territorial expansion of the Soviet areas as much as the growing homogeneity and power of their leadership, were in striking contrast with the increasingly nominal influence of the Shanghai Central Committee. Two additional factors came to accentuate the shift. The Central Committee's fast growing financial dependence on the resources of the Soviet areas was one of them. Then, the successive 'extermination campaigns' launched by the Nationalist Government—by now alarmed over the Communists' growing power—claimed its victims primarily among the urban leaders and decimated those in Shanghai in particular.

In November 1931 when the first All-China Conference of the Soviets met to establish a 'Provisional Central Government of the Chinese Soviet Republics', it had to do so in Juichin, capital of the Soviet areas in Kangsi. The uncontested leader of that area was the same Mao Tse-tung who had been dismissed from the Politburo upon the failure of the Autumn Harvest Rising. And to complete his victory, in the autumn of 1932, seeking refuge from the 'white terror' of the Nationalist Government, the Central Committee itself was forced to leave Shanghai and to move to Juichin.

A provisional Communist government

After 1931, then, an entirely new chapter in the history of Chinese Communism began. From then on it controlled a military force, had a territorial base, and had built on them a dynamic and united governmental machine.

The Soviet areas, of course, depended for their very existence on the skill of the military leaders. The most prominent among them, the one who had already joined Mao in 1928, was Chu Teh. Of the 'urban wing' who had come with the Central Committee, Chou En-lai and Liu Shao-chi were to rise to the highest posts. Yet the man whose ideas and strategy did most to prepare that new chapter was Mao Tse-tung, then recently elected first chairman of the 'Provisional Government' and, already, the uncontested new leader of Chinese Communism.

The rise of Mao Tse-tung

The Chinese Revolution

Born in 1893, Mao Tse-tung was one of the four sons of a Hunanese peasant. His stern father had worked himself out of indebtedness to become the owner of three and a half acres of land. In the poverty of the Hunanese countryside this was enough to mark him off as a relatively 'rich peasant' and to make him want to give his son a respectable education.

Being made to make the traditional trip to the birthplace of Confucius, was only one among Mao's childhood memories contributing to his hatred of the Confucian order. Hunan in China was what Bengal was to India: the cradle of some of the most assertive and the most independent-minded rebels and the home of radical political movements. Memories of famine, local risings and the banditry of the uprooted peasants only reinforced this rebellious disposition. And the stiff conformism of his father helped to turn it into revolt against the established order of things. At fifteen Mao ran away from home, lured by a 'modern' school in a neighbouring county. A few years later he went to college in Changsha, the nearest big city.

The collapse of the monarchy found him there. The student circles of Changsha were naturally agitated by liberal, Socialist and anti-imperialist ideas. Like other keen young men of his generation thirsting for modern knowledge, Mao too absorbed and discarded a succession of 'isms', all the time in search of a creed capable of offering a complete answer to their radical and idealistic aspirations. For half a year he served in the revolutionary army when the rebellion against the Manchu Dynasty began. Later he spent long months touring his native province, familiarizing himself with peasant problems and making his first experiments in organization. Finally, he got a job as assistant librarian in Peking's National Library. There he was in direct contact with the capital's intellectual ferment and he was soon active in the Society for the Study of Marxism at Peking University. Three years later, still only twenty-eight, Mao Tse-tung was among the handful of intellectuals who gathered in Shanghai to found the Chinese Communist Party.

Empirical Marxist

All through these formative years Mao's peasant origin acted like a tenacious root, resisting seduction by abstract theorizing or by urbanized fashions. While his most gifted contemporaries went to study abroad, he had turned down an opportunity to be sent to Paris. Already committed to Marxism, he remained empirical in his awareness that doctrine would have to be adapted to the complex reality of Chinese background and experience. Yet this ruggedly practical aspect of his character was counter-balanced by the strong aesthetic side of his nature. It has repeatedly found expression in poetry which, according to specialists, has been of high quality. But his education in Chinese classics and in modern social theories went hand in hand with an extensive reading of China's great popular novels and of the proletarian literature of past centuries. It is from this source that he has taken the popular quotations and colourful images which sprinkle his writings and speeches and which provide him with a natural bridge to the minds of the people he is addressing.

But the poetic inclination and the practical bent of mind—both recurring features in outstanding Chinese—were completed in Mao's case by two other, major characteristics. The first was his passion for social justice springing from identification with the peasants' sufferings. The second was his capacity to base his decisions on patient observation free of dogmatic assumptions. These, combined with dogged tenacity, were the main ingredients of the colourful and earthy personality which was to make such an impact on Chinese history.

In Hunan he had already won something of a reputation as an organizer. After 1920 he continued the same work among urban workers. But his decisive experience came with the Northern Expedition. At that time, Moscow's instructions called for the 'curbing of excesses' among peasants so as not to jeopardize the chances of continued Kuomintang-Communist collaboration. Thus, somewhat ironically, Mao was attached to the expedition as an agrarian commissar with the mission to temper the extremism of the very peasant associations which the Communist agitators had helped to bring into being. And the fruit of the months Mao had spent with the advancing armies in the Hunanese countryside was a unique document.

The agrarian commissar

The Chinese Revolution

Summing up his impressions and conclusions, he submitted it to the Central Committee of the Communist Party, who refused to publish it. When, finally, a party organ printed it in March 1927, it not merely provided the key to Mao's own position but contained also the germs of the heresy which was to lead the Chinese Communist Party to its final triumph and to make Mao Tse-tung the father of an original Communist strategy.

The author of this *Report on an Investigation of the Agrarian Movement in Hunan* was, at the time, no more than a subordinate member of a party still intent to copy the Russian model and wait for the urban proletariat's opportunity to lead the revolution. Yet the questioning of this strategy was already implicit in Mao's passionate plea. 'The force of the peasantry is like that of the raging winds and driving rain. It is rapidly increasing in violence. No force can stand in its way'—he wrote. 'The peasantry will tear apart all nets which bind it and hasten along the road to liberation. They will bury beneath them all forces of imperialism, militarism, corrupt officialdom, village bosses and evil gentry. Every revolutionary party, every revolutionary comrade will be subjected to their scrutiny and be accepted or rejected by them. Shall we stand in the vanguard and lead them or stand behind them and oppose them? Every Chinese is free to pick his answer. However, destiny will force us to pick an answer soon . . .' he warned.

The role of the peasants
'The broad masses of the peasantry have arisen to fulfil their historic destiny. The democratic forces in the village have arisen to overthrow the feudal forces in the village. The overthrow of feudal forces is, after all, the aim of the national revolution. . . .' This accusing reminder to the address of party leadership, however, was further underscored by an assertion which cast doubt over the fundamental concept of the party line itself, as inspired by the Comintern. 'If we were to compute the relative accomplishment of various elements in the democratic revolution on a percentage basis, the urban dwellers and military would not rate more than thirty per cent, while the remaining seventy per cent would have to be allotted

to the accomplishments of the peasants in the countryside. . . .'

Mao went on to describe as entirely justified the so-called 'excesses' of the peasantry. Nobody, he insisted, was better qualified to distinguish between good and bad gentry. 'The revolution is, after all, no banquet. It's not quite as dainty an occupation as writing books or painting flowers. . . . A revolution is a violent action on the part of one class to overthrow the political power of another. . . . We must build up the vast power of the peasantry.'

Lacking the usual references to Marxist dogma and passionately questioning the sacrosanct assumptions of the official party line, Mao could expect nothing but suspicion from his superiors. Yet this was not his final formula. That the peasantry was not the reactionary force orthodox Communism had believed it to be, was clearly stated. But there was as yet no awareness in his *Report* of the importance of a territorial base nor of the military power needed to back mass support. By insisting on the peasantry's role as the *main force* of revolution, however, Mao Tse-tung had established himself as father of at least a marginal trend within the party. Following the break with the Kuomintang and the failure of the Autumn Harvest Rising, together with the troops which had opted for the Communists he could withdraw to the hills of Chingkanshan and put his ideas into practice. And there he could do so without much effective interference from headquarters in Shanghai.

The result was something quite unprecedented in Chinese history. In the very heart of the country it brought into existence a strong executive power, acting in the name of an ideology, and carrying out revolutionary reforms in face of the central government's opposition.

If Mao, the son of a Hunanese peasant, had a shrewd understanding of the dynamic force of discontent in the countryside, Mao the intellectual was equally aware that no Chinese peasant rising had ever succeeded without leadership by the scholar-officials. The answer was in a disciplined army composed of uprooted peasants but stiffened with Communist refugees from the towns. And if the recruits were promised revenge in the

Organizing
the army

name of the oppressed, the intellectuals who led them aimed higher and were preparing a new social order. The age-old tactics of peasant guerillas were preserved. The Red Army was to avoid frontal attack or static defence. It was to harass the enemy and attack him only when he was already worn out. Above all, it was to reorganize local support wherever it had to act. Inevitably, then, it became the first Chinese army not merely fighting for an ideal but also able to pass on its creed so as to call forth the sympathies of the people among whom it had to fight. Thanks to this novel form of intelligence network the Communists were always well informed of the movements of the Kuomintang troops and were rarely taken by surprise.

As for the reforms, they concerned primarily the ownership of land. It was in the crowded regions of Central China that the evils of landlordism were the most grievous. In some of these areas tenant farmers with no land at all made up over half the rural population. They were exploited both by high rents and by excessive interest rates on the money-lenders' credits. So, in harmony with Mao's diagnosis of peasant anger, the reforms were carried out with ruthless efficiency. The holdings of landlords and of rich peasants were confiscated outright and redistributed among the landless. For the rural gentry in general Communist rule brought a reign of terror. There were frequent executions, even veritable massacres, involving occasionally also political opponents belonging to rival party factions.

Problem for the Kuomintang

Yet it was symptomatic of the prevailing mood of the countryside that notwithstanding such harsh methods, peasant revolution in the Soviet areas struck deep roots. Within the span of a few short years the strength of the Chinese Soviet Republic was such that the Nanking Government had to devote its major military resources to launch a series of offensives to 'suppress the Communist bandits'. For the first time, however, the forces of a Chinese government were facing not just a rival army but also a hostile population defending the advantages it had obtained from a rival authority.

The Kuomintang's police and armed might could fairly easily deal with the urban organizations of the Chinese Communists. But the Soviet areas posed a different problem. Like quicksilver, their forces receded and dissolved before the attackers only to reappear in some fresh sector of armed strength. Though from November 1930 onwards campaign after campaign was launched, not even the vastly superior manpower and equipment of Chiang Kai-shek's forces could make much headway against the rebel Communist régime.

And that, more than any Comintern resolution, offered confirmation that China's Communists had found both the leaders and the methods which—whatever the immediate outcome of the struggle—might decide China's fate in their favour.

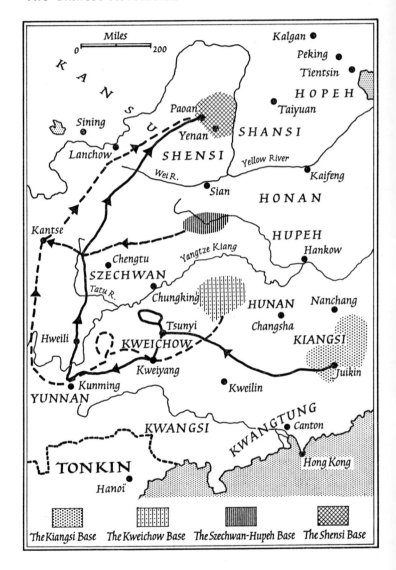

The Long March October 1934–October 1935

The Long March to Yenan

IN 1931 WHEN THE CHINESE SOVIET REPUBLIC was proclaimed with Mao Tse-tung as its President, its authority extended over a fairly large area and over a population of about twenty-five million. Its regular army, composed of nearly 60,000 men in 1931, grew to nearly 300,000 by 1934.

The first Kuomintang offensive launched against the Kiangsi soviets in November 1930 ended in failure before the end of the year. A second one, in the spring of 1931, was not more successful. In July of the same year Chiang Kai-shek personally conducted another campaign at the head of an army of 300,000 men. His efforts being temporarily diverted by Japan's activities in the North, this offensive too, failed. When it was recommenced in the summer of 1932, it managed to liquidate some small Communist bases in Hupeh province, but the fourth offensive directed against the principal Kiangsi base failed.

It was the fifth campaign, begun in October 1933 with 200 aeroplanes and with more than half a million men, that was to be decisive. Numerical superiority and the sheer weight of modern equipment were beginning to tell. Moreover, success was due primarily to the tactics adopted by General Falkenhausen, head of the German military mission at that time advising the Kuomintang. He instituted an inexorable blockade of the Communist-held areas relying on a network of blockhouses able to frustrate well-tried guerilla tactics. This, at last, proved to be effective and by June 1934 Chiang could claim that only three small regions remained infested by Communists and that even those would soon be cleared out.

The Communists realized that the ring was closing around them. Their hope that from Kiangsi they could spread out all over China, lay shattered. To avoid annihilation, and after much deliberation, they decided to abandon Kiangsi, to try to break through the tight blockade, and so to carry with them the Soviet Republic to a new and more secure base.

Chiang's
successful
offensive

109

The Chinese Revolution

Their choice fell on the northern province of Shensi. There, in the great bend of the Yellow River, they knew of the existence of another Communist group. But to get there by the direct route, about 1,200 miles long, would have been impossible. It led across regions where the Kuomintang was in full control. Instead, it was decided to try a roundabout way which would lead through areas where, owing to distance and the difficulty of the terrain, the Kuomintang's control was partial only.

Once the Communists were dislodged from Kiangsi, however, the Kuomintang was triumphant. As in 1927, so in 1934 again, its Press and radio announced the final annihilation of the Communists and the end of the danger they represented for the Nationalist régime.

What really had happened was rather different.

A year's trek   The evacuation of the Kiangsi region began in October 1934. At the cost of some hard fighting the bulk of the Red Army managed to break through the concentric lines of besieging troops. They had to move south-west before they could head westward in the direction of the Tibetan borderlands. Thrown back toward the south, they changed direction and crossed the upper Yangtze. Continuing their northward advance, they again had to fight hard battles in order to cross the Tatu River. Beyond it, following the Szechwan border over difficult mountainous country, the trek led through the north-western Moslem areas and from there over some of the most desolate regions of Kansu province. Finally, about a year after their departure from Kiangsi, the tattered remnants of the Communist armies reached the remote northern part of Shensi. There, at last, they could join up with the guerilla forces in control of the region.

This prodigious feat of endurance became known as the Long March. It involved an organized trek of some 8,000 miles within a year. It led across eleven provinces, over remote regions inhabited by suspicious peoples, through murderous marshy lands overgrown by grass, and in face of continuous danger from local and governmental forces. It is claimed that the three Communist armies who participated in the march crossed eighteen mountain chains and twenty-four large rivers, broke through the armies of ten war-lords, defeated dozens of Kuomintang regiments, and took temporarily sixty-two cities.

The basic aim, to save the revolution, was thus achieved. But the price was heavy. Of the 130,000 men who had left Kiangsi and Hunan, less than 30,000 arrived in North Shensi. Some deserted on the way intimidated by hardship. Many more perished in battle or succumbed to fatigue, frost, or to the other rigours of a hostile nature. Of several hundred women, no more than thirty survived. Among those who perished was Mao Tse-tung's wife. But those who reached Shensi constituted a hard core of tempered steel, a reliable and disciplined force with which to build the new Soviet Republic.

Three factors connected with the Long March were to help that task.

The first concerned Communist prestige. The Kuomintang continued to claim that the Communists had succumbed and ceased to represent any threat. Its Press was tightly controlled and public opinion was preoccupied with Japan's moves so that few people were aware of the historic events in the remote interior of the country. Yet the epic story of the Long March was fast growing into a legend. Its incidents became the themes of songs and stories. Slowly what really had happened became known and the heroes of such a performance could hardly be described any longer as the unprincipled bandits of the Kuomintang's propaganda. On the contrary, a new prestige, springing from the admiration due to national heroes, was beginning to surround the Communists' enterprise.

The second factor was the new, total cohesion of the Communist Party. Next to the Kiangsi Soviet there had existed other Communist-controlled areas and not all of them had been unconditional in their acceptance of Mao's leadership. As the various groups had joined up with the Long March, a number of political meetings had been held on the way which gradually helped to eliminate existing differences. By the time the Communists reached their destination, the military and political

The march becomes a legend

leaders had won unanimous support and Mao Tse-tung's 'line' and leadership of the party emerged uncontested.

The third factor was the human experience the Long March had provided. Like an involuntary and monumental study tour, it splendidly completed the Communists' already unrivalled knowledge of the Chinese peasant's psychology. It brought them into contact with new regions and different peoples. Disseminating their ideas among them on their way, they also learnt a great deal about the problems and the attitudes of masses they were destined to govern later on. As a significant by-product of this experience, for the first time, the Long March brought the Communists into direct contact with the 'national minorities' of the south-west and of the western regions and rendered both sides conscious of their ideas and aims.

Establishing the base

Thus, with their moral stature grown but physically and numerically weakened, the Communists began to organize their new base.

After a pause, partly spent in negotiations with the local revolutionaries, an attempt was made to bring more territory under the Communists' control. In December 1936 the small town of Yenan was taken and for several years to come it served as the capital of the new Soviet Republic.

The area chosen was less easily accessible to the Kuomintang forces than had been Kiangsi. Also, as in Chingkanshan, this was once again a border area falling into several provincial jurisdictions and thus rendering the action of the local, provincial authorities less effective. Yet the problems to be faced were enormous. The region was poor and sparsely populated. Food was scarce. So were recruits for the fighting forces or the arms they needed.

So it was in an atmosphere of general austerity, and practically ignored by the outside world, that once again the Communists began to build up their base into a veritable social laboratory.

The Alternative

FOR SOME TIME AFTER THE LONG MARCH the world knew little about what was really going on in Yenan. The few reports brought out by foreigners—Edgar Snow's *Red Star Over China* foremost among them—spoke of interesting social experiments and of the ascetic simplicity and the romantic privations of the new régime. All this, of course, tended to establish its fame and enhance its moral standing.

The country surrounding the new capital of Chinese Communism consisted of loess hills and for a long time troops and leaders alike lived in caves carved out of them. A simple journal, the *Liberation Daily*, was edited in the town's Temple of Ten Thousand Buddhas. There were agrarian, political and educational reforms. A university, functioning under spartan conditions, provided political and military education with special attention paid to the art of guerilla warfare. And the quality of the teaching was such that young men and even officers were beginning to come to it from all over the country. But the area controlled by the Communists was small. It was bleak, it had no real contact with the towns, and its population barely surpassed one million.

Gradually, however, the new Soviet began to spread. The Red Army was steadily built up and its guerilla tactics in skirmishes with governmental and Japanese troops served to broaden Communist influence. Contacts with the rest of China developed. Step by step small industries were acquired, simple arms were manufactured, and daily existence took on a slightly more organized form. Above all, the number of students and intellectuals who were coming to Yenan was on the increase.

Though the new base was still precarious, it attracted more sympathy and support from non-Communist Chinese than Juichin ever did. The explanation was to be found in the growing frustration caused by the Kuomintang's performance, and in the Communists' completely changed policies.

The Chinese Revolution

Disillusionment with the Nationalists grows

The first constructive élan of the Nationalist Government appeared to be exhausted. A widening fringe of failure and injustice forming around the system's edges was in sharp contrast with Yenan's purposeful self-assurance. While the Communists were concentrating their efforts on giving social and economic content to their programme, it had become clear that the Kuomintang was incapable of giving any practical meaning to the People's Livelihood principle however much lip-service it had been paying to Sun Yat-sen's teachings. Above all, the conclusion seemed to be justified that the Nationalist Government had neither the desire nor the power to face the all-important land problem. How blind the Kuomintang leadership was to the gravity of this problem was tragically illustrated by its decisions after the Communists had been dislodged from Kiangsi.

Restoration of the landlords

There, a clear choice was placed before it. Either it had to confirm the land redistribution programme and the other revolutionary changes which the Communists had carried out, or it had to annul them and return the land to the former landlords. Nanking opted for the restoration of the landlords' rights and for a return to conditions as they had existed before the Kiangsi Soviet. This, naturally, played directly into the hands of the Communists. It helped to confirm their propaganda and alienated the masses still further.

Furthermore, the growing sterility of the Kuomintang's social policies had been accompanied by the simultaneous liberalization of some Communist methods. This was due to several causes, most of them practical and little to do with ideological considerations.

To begin with, the agrarian problems of North Shensi were very different from those prevailing in Kiangsi. The proportion of tenant farmers with no land of their own was much smaller than in Central China. Nor was exploitation through high rents and excessive interest rates comparable to practices in the overcrowded regions of the south. For all these reasons the peasantry in the north was much less responsive to the kind of incitement and call for armed rebellion than had been the peasants in Kiangsi. Greater tolerance towards landlords and a programme for the reduction of rents and interest rates were likely to yield more promising results.

Such milder agrarian policies may also have become necessary in order to erase the memories of the mass-executions and the other excesses of the Kiangsi days; harsh methods which had frightened away many potential supporters. But the decisive reason for the more tolerant approach was the Communists' urgent desire to acquire a wider social base. It was only through such a broadening of their support within China that they could hope to expand their modest territorial base and to build up the reservoir of strength which they needed if they were to be able to challenge the Nationalist Government's authority. The common denominator most likely to serve these ends was the call to patriotism and for unity to face the menace of Japanese aggression.

The Communists realized that in order to put an end to their austere and threatened existence, they would have to spread out over the plains of North China where they could find the human and material means of ultimate success. For the time being, however, they were far too weak to confront the Nationalists' armed might. To realize their aim they either had to compel Chiang Kai-shek to fight on two fronts—against the Communists and against Japan—or force him to fight the Japanese in alliance with them.

A choice of tactics

The first, to force Chiang to fight both the internal and the external enemy, appeared hardly realizable. Yet Chiang was conscious of the dilemma facing him. He knew that all-out war against Japan would expose the Kuomintang to the Communists' threat. To fight both simultaneously, he knew to be beyond his means. Moreover, aware as he was of the danger Japan represented, his obsession with Communism easily convinced him that first he had to finish with them and turn against the Japanese only after. He may have argued that China was still too weak to take on Japan and so she had to offer concessions in order to buy time. In the meantime, so he had hoped, the Kuomintang ought to dispose of the Communists in its rear. As for the Japanese, it was not in their interest that the Nationalist Government should consolidate its power and so they kept up their pressure, continuing to mutilate and to humiliate China. The net result of all this was Nanking's continued passivity in face of Japanese belligerence; growing discontent among patriotic Chinese; and renewed 'extermination campaigns' against the Yenan régime.

An alliance against the Japanese?

Clearly, then, the Communists had to turn to their second alternative: to try to compel Chiang to fight Japan with their aid. Simply to convince him to do so seemed hopeless. It was only by mobilizing patriotic public opinion that pressure could be brought on him. The class struggle and the agrarian revolution having appropriately been toned down, propaganda was focused on the issue of resistance against Japan's creeping conquest. The Communist line was consistent. In 1932 already the newly established Chinese Soviet Republic had gone on record with a somewhat platonic declaration of war against Japan. Manifestoes calling for action had been issued at regular intervals during the next two years. Now, in August 1935, Yenan issued a call to the nation again demanding a united national front to oppose Japan.

'Chinese don't fight Chinese'

These appeals and their accompanying propaganda found a wide echo all over the country. Their effect was only heightened by Japan's endless claims and by Chiang's continued acquiescence in the extension of her rights and domination all over North China. While informed public opinion grew more and more impatient with continued civil war, slogans were suitably adapted. If *Unification before Resistance* was Nanking's motto, the much more effective *Chinese don't Fight Chinese* was Yenan's reply. Yet the north-western armies were preparing for further drives against North Shensi and, accordingly, the mobilization of public opinion had to be stepped up. Following another attempt by the Kuomintang armies to destroy the Shensi Soviet in November 1935, a series of demonstrations swept the country. This, the so-called 'December 9, 1935, Movement' started off with a large student demonstration in Peking, repeated again a week later, which called for an end to civil

116

war and for unity against the Japanese. They led to bloody repression. Similar clashes occurred in a number of other towns and, appropriately timed, they were soon followed by a message from Mao Tse-tung to Nanking promising to recognize the Kuomintang's leadership in exchange for renewed collaboration with the Communists.

Followed by no positive measures, the Communists were pushing their propaganda into top gear. Synchronized with other demands for a united front, they were beginning to influence fast growing masses of people and to such an extent that the new mood was beginning to strain the loyalty of even some of the fighting units of the Kuomintang armies.

Gradually, the Communists were succeeding in their aim to whip up a massive body of support. Moreover, they were beginning to deprive the Kuomintang of its exclusive 'nationalist' label and to emerge in the eyes of many as the spokesmen of authentic Chinese patriotic sentiment. This was bringing them genuine advantages in the form of diminishing isolation, wider sympathies among all classes, and of even greater direct support. In fact, the nationalist appeal, the new moderation of their revolutionary programme, together with the Kuomintang's decay and Chiang's temporization, helped to turn Yenan in the eyes of many Chinese into the sole practical alternative to Nanking's rule.

Yet great as the successes of the united front propaganda had been, the ultimate aim, renewed Kuomintang-Communist collaboration, was not much nearer. Chiang remained adamant and it became clear that the campaign for a united front had to be reinforced, if need be even through bold and desperate means.

The need for haste

Their own considerations apart, the Chinese Communists' haste was also inspired by the international context. Hitler had been in power for three years. The Comintern's anxiety—already apparent in its resolution in the Summer of 1935—was turning into alarm after the signature of the anti-Comintern pact in November 1936. In face of the growing menace represented by the Axis Powers, the hour of Popular Fronts had arrived in Europe and in Asia. In the Kremlin's perspective the Kuomintang was still China's dominant political force and Chiang Kai-shek the national leader. It was with them that the Chinese Communists could most effectively oppose Japan. And if for all these reasons the Chinese Communist Party was now determined to force the issue, Japan's increasingly aggressive attitude was certainly helping their cause.

Towards a United Front

EVER SINCE THEIR VICTORY OVER RUSSIA, the Japanese had been methodically consolidating their influence in Manchuria. Being a large and sparsely populated area rich in natural resources, it had traditionally attracted the interest of the powers along its borders. Russian influence in Manchuria had been in decline after 1905. Since the fall of the Monarchy no Chinese central government managed to establish effective control over it. As for the Japanese, entrenched in their leasehold in Dairen and Port Arthur, their interests had grown more and more widespread.

During the first three decades of this century the Japanese invested much effort and a great deal of capital in the economic development of Manchuria, particularly in power production, in rail and river communications, in mines, and in heavy industry. Though few Japanese migrants were tempted because of the severe climate, Japanese business administrators, military personnel and technicians found important work in Manchuria and in large numbers. Japan's population and industry were fast expanding and the need for overseas possessions offering food and raw materials at advantageous terms, was becoming pressing. Manchuria was offering all those advantages.

The railway network of South Manchuria was connected with that of North China and after 1911 millions of Chinese farmers were moving in over those lines in search of better living. The original Manchu population was rapidly turned into a small minority. Simultaneously, agricultural production increased steadily as Chinese immigrants opened up new land and Manchuria's crops had become important in regional trade. The mines provided Japan with much-needed raw materials and Manchurian heavy industry became vital to Japan's economic and military modernization. Gradually, then, South Manchuria was turned into a virtual commercial monopoly of

Japan monopolizes South Manchuria

119

Japan, providing also a base for her projected territorial expansion.

Legally, China was the controlling power. But in practice Japan made the real decisions. In 1915 the Japanese forced China to extend their twenty-five-year lease to ninety-nine years. Their investments, as much as the activities of their military men, were steadily growing. Moreover, hundreds of thousands of Koreans—Japanese subjects since 1910—were pouring across the Yalu River in search of employment in the still under-populated Manchuria. In face of this combined economic and military position, neither the power of the local war-lords nor the authority of the Nanking Government could any longer counter-balance Japan's pressure.

Subjects of dispute were not lacking. Unwilling to recognize the enforced extension of the Japanese lease on Dairen and Port Arthur, Nanking claimed that it had expired in 1923. The Japanese insisted that the new arrangement was binding and should last till 1997. There was friction also in connection with Japanese rights in the zone of the South Manchurian Railway; over who had the right to levy taxes within it, or whether the Japanese could maintain their own railway guards. Also Japan was irritated by the obstacles the Chinese had placed upon the acquisition of properties by Koreans and Japanese. Finally, the Chinese intended to build new railways in Manchuria, some of which would have paralleled the Japanese-controlled lines and thus would have endangered Japan's virtual monopoly of trade in the regions concerned. While these problems had been under constant negotiation between Japanese and Chinese officials, there occurred also political changes which tended to reinforce the arguments of Japanese extremists who were calling for decisive action.

Patriotic
sentiment

Five times the size of Great Britain, Manchuria had a frontier tradition making her people impatient of control by distant authorities not familiar with their immediate problems. Yet at the same time they were patriotic Chinese and they regarded their province as an advance post of their country's security. They resented Japanese encroachments in the form of special treaties and economic concessions, just as much as the rest of China disliked similar foreign privileges. Moreover, far from being a backward frontier region, Manchuria was in many ways China's most developed area especially in terms of industrial progress.

Between 1927 and 1930 when the Nanking Government was actively pursuing the unification of the country, Chang Tso-lin was in effective control of Manchuria. After his death in 1928, his son Chang Hsueh-liang, 'the Young Marshal' succeeded him with apparently pro-Japanese policies. About the same time a coalition of northern war-lords were defying Nanking's authority and proceeded to form a rival government. In 1930 when Chiang Kai-shek attempted to disperse the rebels, he succeeded only because the Young Marshal had come to his rescue. Influenced, perhaps, by the country-wide nationalist and anti-Japanese sentiment, the Young Marshal may have come to the conclusion that the time had arrived to side with the central government. The Nationalist flag was hoisted in Manchuria in October 1930. But seeing that the most consistently separatist provinces of China were ready to acknowledge the authority of the Nanking Government and thus to identify Manchuria with the rest of the country, the Japanese felt that they could wait no longer.

In the night of 18 September 1931, an explosion shook the city of Mukden. The Japanese claimed that it had been caused by a Chinese attempt to blow up the tracks of the Chinese Eastern Railway. Although a train passed unhurt after the mysterious explosion, the 'incident' served to justify retaliation in the form of the lightning invasion of the three Eastern Provinces or, in other words, of the complete elimination of all Chinese authority from the whole of Manchuria. Chiang Hsieh-liang's troops—among the best equipped in China—being away participating in the blockade of the Communist areas in Shensi, the military occupation of Manchuria was completed without any serious resistance.

The Mukden incident

A few months later Japan's new possession was transformed into a puppet-state under the name of Manchukuo. From their

'Manchukuo'

Concession in Tientsin, the Japanese produced the last Emperor of the Manchu Dynasty, Pu Yi, who had been living there since his removal from Peking in 1924, and made him ruler of the new State. Later on they even promoted him to the rank of Emperor of Manchukuo, meaning Manchu Empire. In September 1932 they recognized its 'independence' and signed with it a treaty of alliance for joint defence. The whole operation, of course, was claimed to be spontaneous and in response to popular demand. But it was too clumsy to be convincing. With the aid of Japanese 'advisers', with their economic control complete, and with the open encouragement given to the revival of Confucian tradition, it served merely to turn Japan's privileged position in North-east China into outright occupation.

Nor was Japanese aggression restricted to Manchuria alone. An effective boycott of Japanese goods and business interests in Shanghai had been going on for some time before the Mukden incident. Following the invasion of Manchuria it became even more severe. The municipal authorities having failed to give satisfaction to Japanese demands to dissolve the boycott committees, Japan landed marines. In the ensuing fighting there were heavy casualties and the city was very seriously damaged. Three days later, on 1 February 1932, Japanese gunboats also bombarded Nanking.

All these events, however, were merely the external projections of important developments within Japan and in the international situation as a whole.

The parliamentary practices existing in Japan since 1922 tended to render public opinion more articulate and, to that extent, to obstruct the projects of the militarists and of their civilian sympathizers. To arrest China's march toward unity offered an opportunity also to put an end to democratic political institutions at home. When, after careful planning, Manchuria was occupied, the 'state of emergency' created within Japan enabled the military and civilian imperialists to liquidate the democratic experiment and so to combine fascism at home with imperialism abroad.

Towards a United Front

In its wider, international context the occupation of Man-churia was merely the first link in the chain of events which, through the rise of Hitler and the destruction of the League of Nations, was ultimately to lead to the Second World War.

For nearly a century it had been accepted in the West that China was 'the sick man of Asia'; that she was disunited and that the Chinese were temperamentally incapable of running an efficient government or maintaining law and order. Such generalizations helped to advance the views of certain powerful interests not unsympathetic to the rise of fascism both in Europe and Asia. According to such views, as applied to the Far East, in place of the old practice of a Chinese strong man acting in western interests, it might now be more convenient to substitute the idea of a strong country able to control China and willing to share its profits with the West. Free of foreign control, China might become an unruly country and might even upset the balance of world power. The political future thus being uncertain, it might be better to accept limited profits by investing in Japan and so reduce direct risks.

The arguments advanced and the propaganda built upon them by Japan, were not unlike those Hitler was to employ later on concerning Czechoslovakia. China was described as likely to spread the Communist infection in Asia, just as Hitler later presented the role of Czechoslovakia. The same people who accepted the occupation of Manchuria as a prelude to direct conflict between Japan and the Soviet Union, were later to consider that the invasion of Czechoslovakia was bringing nearer the day of a German–Soviet clash. If it was hoped that war between Russia and Germany would leave the West the arbiter, war between Japan and Russia promised to permit the West to recover its old supremacy in the Far East.

Under these circumstances it was barely surprising that the reaction of the western powers and of the League of Nations was less than effective. Trusting the West's revulsion in face of Japanese aggression, immediately after the Mukden 'incident' China appealed to the League of Nations and urged the United States—not a member of the League—to lend her support.

The Chinese Revolution

No sanctions
applied

The obvious disinclination to apply armed sanctions was at least partly justified by two considerations. The United States like the rest of the West were in the midst of the Great Depression and were understandably preoccupied with their own economic problems. Moreover, thanks to the dispositions of the 1922 Washington Treaty, neither the USA nor Great Britain commanded adequate naval strength in the Far East, while Japan controlled the approaches to the Manchurian and Chinese coasts. At the time of a grave domestic crisis, then, armed sanctions would have involved the western powers in a costly and probably long war against an enemy whose fleet controlled what would have been the main theatre of hostilities.

In January 1932, by what came to be known as the Stimson Doctrine, the Americans refused to recognize Manchukuo and their example was followed by the majority of the League's members. In May of the same year the League despatched to Manchuria an international commission headed by Lord Lytton presumably to report the obvious, namely the *fait accompli* of the conquest. Its recommendation of an autonomous Manchuria was accepted by the League of Nations in February 1933 and completed by a call to Japan to refrain from military action in China. Japan's answer was that not she but 'independent' Manchukuo was responsible for whatever further action followed. And to demonstrate the importance she attached to the warning, in March 1933 Japan left the League of Nations.

If, as the Americans had insisted, the Open Door policy emerged from the Manchurian 'incident' unimpaired, the League of Nations had been mortally wounded. The first power which openly defied the world order and the peace machinery established after the First World War, received only half-hearted, verbal reprimands. The conclusions were quickly drawn. Hitler rose to power in Germany. Italy attacked Ethiopia. Fascism was forced on Spain with overt German and Italian complicity. What began with the Mukden explosion was remorselessly snow-balling into the Second World War.

Japan
consolidates
her hold

Japan, originator of these developments, was, of course, not slow to exploit their lesson for her own advantage. Through

124

the fiction of Manchukuo, she went on to consolidate her economic and political hold of North-east China. Although in May 1932 she suspended her military action in Shanghai, she prepared more important moves in the North. In 1933 the Japanese struck at the Chinese province of Jehol, just north of Peking. About half the size of France, they occupied it in ten days. They did so by the use of motorized units on a scale unknown in modern warfare. And their innovation probably served as an example to German strategists who were soon to reproduce it under ominously symmetrical conditions against Czechoslovakia first and against Poland later on.

With Jehol occupied, the Japanese went on to extend their control westward through Inner Mongolia, and southward into the north-eastern provinces of China, including Peking and the great port of Tientsin. Clearly, the Japanese were by now determined to turn all China into the kind of puppet-state they had created in Manchuria. With that aim before them, and relying on their strategic reserves, they were employing a mixture of political and economic pressure.

To begin with, they systematically wrecked the economy of North China. Their main instrument to do so was organized and large-scale smuggling often under the protection of the military. The goods which thus flooded North China had paid no duty and so deprived the government of part of its customs on foreign trade, the decisive item in China's national revenue. Chinese industry and trade suffered greatly. Significantly, heroin and opium, intended to hasten demoralization, were prominent among the goods smuggled in and then distributed by Japanese and Korean vendors.

The resulting economic chaos helped to pave the way for political penetration. True to their past practice, the Japanese acted piecemeal. They negotiated with one local commander before turning to the other, or to the authorities for confirmation or for further concessions. But gradually incessant pressure was to crystallize into a wider political design. The wish was expressed that the five northern provinces of Shantung, Honan, Suiyuan, Shansi and Hopeh be recognized as constituting a

Political penetration

special region with 'legitimate aspirations' of its own. The demand followed that Nanking should agree to the setting up of a 'political council' for the area, through which it could deal with the Japanese. The logical next step was to ask that the personnel of this 'North China Political Council' be acceptable to the Japanese. The basic aim, of course, was to establish that local interests were superior to national ones and so to arrest progress toward unification.

Through such and similar methods the Japanese succeeded in severing North China from the rest of the country. And wishing to profit from the crisis in Europe, they did not intend to stop. But Chiang Kai-shek was still determined to avoid a head-on collision with Japan and continued to trade space for time. In the meantime he continued to be preoccupied with the Communists and directed the armies under Chang Hsueh-liang—withdrawn from Manchuria—to attack them in their North Shensi stronghold.

But by this time patriotic Chinese public opinion was growing impatient with Chiang's appeasement of the Japanese. Demonstrations by university students were attracting much sympathy. Moreover, the insistent Communist call for a united front against the common enemy was beginning to find an echo even among the Kuomintang's own troops.

The Sian Incident

IT WAS AGAINST SUCH A BACKGROUND that a totally unexpected and highly dramatic event occurred destined to change the course of the Chinese Revolution.

On 4 December 1936, Chiang Kai-shek arrived in Sian personally to investigate a crisis of discipline among his commanders. Sian dominated the strategic plain below the Communists' base in Shensi. It was also the headquarters of the Manchurian armies just ordered to prepare another campaign against the Communists. For some time past there had been reports that Chang Hsueh-liang, their commander, was in disagreement with the Generalissimo's policy of 'Unification before Resistance' and at points along the front his troops began even to fraternize with the Communists. With his customary disregard for his personal safety, Chiang went straight to the centre of the trouble to put matters right.

After eight days of negotiations there was open mutiny and on December 12 Chang Hsueh-liang arrested Chiang Kai-shek. An attempt was made to force him to accept a sweeping settlement of all political and military issues and to obtain his promise to fight the Japanese before the Communists. The Generalissimo refused to yield and his courage and his fanatical self-confidence appeared to have impressed even his captors.

Chang Hsueh-liang's North-eastern armies were not the only troops present. Local provincial troops were also stationed around the city and they were neither well disciplined nor clearly under the orders of the Nanking Government. The Red Army was not far away in the North and there were some Kuomintang troops within striking distance. Each one of these, surrounded, outflanked or counter-balanced by the combination of the other forces, there existed a precarious equilibrium with Chiang Kai-shek's life in the balance.

Expecting his summary execution, Chiang was informed instead that an emissary of the Communists had arrived and

The arrest of Chiang Kai-shek

that negotiations would begin again. The delegate from Yenan was Chou En-lai, the most resilient and certainly the most gifted negotiator of the Communists. As a result of his intervention, and after long debates, the Kuomintang leader's humiliating captivity came to an end on Christmas Day. He yielded to the officers' demands, agreed to resume collaboration with the Communists, interrupted since 1927, and he emerged with his prestige enhanced as the acknowledged leader of all China in the anti-Japanese war. Yet at Chiang's insistence, Chang Hsueh-liang, the very general who kidnapped him, was to accompany him back to Nanking. There he was to be tried by court-martial as a mutineer, was imprisoned and finally disappeared.

Agreement with the Communists

Under the terms of the agreement outlined in Sian, the Communists gave up their claim to independence and agreed to be considered simply as an autonomous Border Area Administration. Their forces were to be reorganized as the Eighth Route Army of the national forces and be placed under the strategic command of Chiang himself. As for the Generalissimo, he was not only liberated with his prestige unimpaired but he was also confirmed by all concerned as the undisputed national leader. In exchange he consented merely to be the head and the symbol of patriotic resistance against the invader. Seeing what appeared to be a *coup d'état* to end in agreement between the antagonists, there was relief in the country and even a sense of national achievement. Impending tragedy had been turned into a satisfying confirmation that, after more than two decades of civil strife, national unity against external danger was at last restored.

Superficially, then, China had come through a grave crisis with her purpose clarified. In view of later developments, however, different interpretations have been given to this curious incident.

What really happened?

According to one side what had happened was a simple and cynical extortion case, a Communist plot in two stages. First they had infiltrated and contaminated the North-eastern Army and then they resorted to a coldly calculated plot to force the Generalissimo to accept the Communists' terms under the threat of death.

Others believe that much that happened in Sian had been unforeseen. Though stimulated by the Communists' united front propaganda, the mutiny of the troops may have been spontaneous, especially as their home country had been the first victim of Japan's aggression. As for the Communists' intervention on behalf of Chiang Kai-shek, his leadership was still indispensable to preserve national unity and his elimination at that stage would have been disastrous both for the Communists and for China as a whole. The Communists, so the argument runs, still needed time to build up their strength. By standing forth as champions of national resistance even at the cost of temporary sacrifices, they were to gain the support of patriotic opinion as well as the physical possibility to exploit collaboration with Nanking for their own territorial expansion.

Truth may be somewhere half-way. Even if the Communists are formally absolved from complicity in the actual kidnapping, it followed shortly after the truce they had established with the mutinous troops. Had they not saved Chiang's life, it is unlikely that his successor would have had the power or the inclination to make the decision to devote all the Nanking Government's means to war against the external enemy only. Also there was the international situation. Hitler was rearming west of the Soviet Union. In the East, Japan was creeping along the borders of Siberia. Stalin still believed that the Kuomintang and not the Communists were the decisive force in China. So, whatever influence the Comintern still had over Mao Tse-tung it was certainly exerted in favour of collaboration and of unity in face of Japan.

Whichever of these interpretations is the correct one, the Sian compromise became the turning point in the history of modern China, and Japan could not have failed to draw the necessary conclusions.

A turning point

Daily, her planes had been circling over China's cities, flying low to intimidate the population with the bombs visible in their racks. Japanese troops were scattered all over North China.

The Chinese Revolution

Now, this dramatic demonstration of the new mood and of the psychological cohesion of the Chinese masses was threatening to foil Japan's aim to bring all China under her domination through regional pressures and through piecemeal aggression. The hour of choice was approaching for Japan. Either she had to back down or resolve to make war on a large scale.

Two months after Chiang Kai-shek left Sian, and while the military operations against the Communists had ceased, the Central Committee of the Chinese Communist Party had drawn up the text of its detailed propositions for renewed collaboration with the Kuomintang. The final document, to serve as the chart of the anti-Japanese united front, was completed in the first week of July. Three days later, on 7 July 1937, Japanese soldiers began to shoot at the Marco Polo bridge just outside Peking.

War with
Japan

Planned as a local incident only, it was one in the long chain of provocation and intimidation serving the aim to convert indirect Japanese control in North China into open military occupation. But the fighting got out of hand because of the unexpected reaction of the Chinese soldiers on the spot. The revolt of Chinese opinion against appeasement and the rising popular anger with Japan had been further intensified by the psychological impact of the united front agreement born in Sian.

The Chinese decision to fight back may have been taken by local officers under pressure from their own men. Yet resistance spread like wildfire and in the ensuing hostilities the Chinese soldiers fought with a hitherto unknown determination. There were cases where officers who had abandoned their troops later returned to them seeing them fighting on without their guidance. There was a new feeling that the country was engaged in a fight for survival, and the indiscriminate slaughter by the superior arms of the Japanese merely helped to inflame hatred and to stiffen resistance.

Within a few days the war with Japan began in earnest. From the comparatively minor clash at the Marco Polo bridge, it rapidly developed into large-scale hostilities. Thus, barely six months after the Sian incident, what had been a limited conflict since 1931 had now broadened into a long and general war.

Chiang Kai-shek never ceased to consider the Sian deal as the greatest mistake of his life. Against his convictions, he was forced to turn from the domestic to the external enemy. This certainly upset his plans in building China's political future. But it did not alter his faith in the ultimate success of China's cause.

In his own, characteristic fashion the Generalissimo had clearly foreseen what was at stake. 'It goes without saying that we are unable to put up a successful resistance to Japan . . . [they] have made the necessary military preparations and are able to invade China . . . but she does not possess enough strength to . . . bring the world under her domination'—he said in 1934 in a lecture to his officers. 'Under such circumstances our military men must pay special attention to the changes in the international situation as well as those in the domestic situation. . . . If we could strengthen ourselves, we would find friends all over the world. No matter how powerful Japan is militarily, she is already placed in isolation. . . . With the attainment of complete unity, in the case of world war breaking out, it might not be necessary for us to face our enemy on the battlefield as victory diplomatically and strategically would already have been ours. . . .'

Except that he now had to face the enemy on the battlefield, this was a farsighted and realistic diagnosis. Understandably, however, the Generalissimo overlooked one possibility. It was that the victory so gained might not be his but rather that of his domestic enemies whom he had tried but had failed to destroy.

Chiang's
prediction

Part Four

Towards Pearl Harbour

JAPAN'S MILITARY INCURSIONS in Asia have played a fateful role in modern history. In 1895 her war against China sealed the fate of the Chinese monarchy. Japan's victory over Russia in 1905 undermined the Tsars. Then, during the Second World War, by taking over Europe's empires in Asia she rendered inevitable the decolonization of the post-war years and thus the final emancipation of the continent she had wished to dominate. Yet perhaps none of these interventions had more far-reaching consequences than the one that began in 1937 at the Marco Polo bridge. It was to mark the beginning of the last act of the Chinese Revolution.

If there existed any possibility for the Kuomintang to carry out indispensable reforms and to consolidate its hold over most of China, the war imposed by Japan interrupted the process. Her blockade and occupation strangled China's economy. They cut her off almost completely from the outside world. To resist in order to survive, came to dominate all other problems before the Chinese. It was a challenge that called for a strategy which had to be military, social and political at the same time.

To answer that challenge two entirely different and incompatible conceptions emerged. Each represented wholly different ideas and methods how resistance could or should be organized. The very nature of these two conceptions rendered henceforth lasting compromise between Kuomintang and Communists impossible. One of the two had to triumph. And the one that triumphed would emerge from the war strong enough to rule post-war China.

Up to 1937 the Japanese hoped to avoid all-out war on the continent. For six years, following the Mukden incident, they advanced step by step, creating subservient local administrations on their way and hoping that, ultimately, they could bring into being for all China the kind of puppet régime they had set up in Manchukuo.

Full-scale war   But the growing success of the united front agitation, the unity produced by the Sian agreement and, finally, the resulting and unexpected bellicosity of the Chinese soldiers changed the situation radically. Although the Marco Polo bridge incident was followed by the usual apologies on behalf of the local authorities, popular anger was uncontrollable and crowds of infuriated Chinese were beginning to attack Japanese in Shanghai and in the other big cities.

Clearly, Japan had to choose between a complete retreat from the course she had been pursuing since 1931, and the decision to undertake the full-scale invasion of China. This was by no means unwelcome to certain elements in Japan. Radical militarists, backed by important financial and business interests, had been pressing the Japanese Government for a more intransigent foreign policy. To these men, the course pursued in China seemed over-cautious. A wave of political assassinations during the previous years had been intended to give weight to their demand for a more aggressive attitude and their influence was rapidly growing. Evidently the moment was not one for compromise in China. The challenge was taken up with relish. Within a few days the full-scale invasion of China began.

As a matter of routine the Japanese had been concentrating overwhelming military power at strategic points so as to be able to crush local resistance if it should break out. In addition, the Japanese Air Force dominated the skies uncontested. Understandably, then, the advance of the Japanese invasion was rapid. By the end of July they had seized Peking. They also advanced in Inner Mongolia and in Shansi, quickly extending their occupation over most of North China. Almost simultaneously, jealous of the army's victories, the Japanese navy attempted to take Shanghai. But notwithstanding a merciless bombardment, thousands of marines were lost in frontal assaults without decisive results. Chinese resistance was unexpectedly vigorous and only the arrival of the Japanese army could finally decide the outcome of the battle. In November 1937 Shanghai too was abandoned. Once beyond the city, the Japanese could exploit their immense superiority in mechanized

136

equipment, in the air and in firing power, and their advance toward Nanking was fast. When the Japanese entered the capital before the end of the year, they celebrated their victory with a reign of terror that lasted several weeks. The looting, rape, arson, and the massacre of military prisoners and civilians occurred on such a scale that world public opinion reacted with shocked horror. That long and terrible halt in Nanking, however, provided the Chinese forces with an unexpected respite. From that moment onward Japan's offensive moved into a lower gear.

The capital was hastily moved to Hankow on the Yangtze while the Japanese columns began to thrust again, this time farther to the south. Their aim was to advance along the two vertical railway systems connecting the Yellow River valley with that of the Yangtze. During this second phase of the invasion, having regained their breath, the Chinese armies were beginning to resort to systematic delaying operations comparable on a smaller scale to the tactics Russia was to adopt later on in face of Hitler's invasion. This strategy of defence in depth permitted the mechanized spearheads of the Japanese armies to thrust ahead until their communication lines became sufficiently vulnerable to be attacked on their flank. The success of this kind of defence, however, was seriously handicapped by the presence of Japanese warships on the Yangtze. The river is so deep and wide that even large cruisers can steam all the way up to Hankow in the centre of China. The Chinese front, though never really broken even when in retreat, was repeatedly turned along the river, forcing renewed and hurried withdrawals. This way the Japanese navy enabled the land forces to reach Hankow by October 1938, and almost simultaneously Canton too was occupied.

So, after little over a year of undeclared war, Japan dominated North China and the great belly of the country east of the line running almost straight from Peking through Hankow down to Canton. This meant that Japan controlled the principal cities and all the ports. It meant also that practically the whole railway network of the country was under Japanese

Defence in depth

control. Moreover, more than half of China's population lived east of that line, there were China's richest agricultural regions, almost all the existing industries, and most of the well-developed coal mines.

The move to Chungking

A few months after the fall of Hankow, Chiang Kai-shek and the Nationalist Government were once again on the move. This time they were retreating deep into the interior, to the city of Chungking, in Szechwan. Being west of the Yangtze Gorges, it was beyond the reach of the Japanese navy. Surrounded by mountains and far from any railway, it offered security against land attack. But the part of China that remained under the Nationalists' rule was economically the most backward. Its industrial production was negligible, it was almost entirely without railways, and whatever roads there existed were in a deplorable condition. Moreover, with the Japanese navy controlling the coast and the Yangtze River, no supplies could reach it either by sea or by rail. The only exceptions were a small trickle coming in through Indo-China (sealed off when the Japanese moved in there in 1940), the truck-road from Burma, and the 2,000-mile route across Sinkiang from the Soviet Union.

Such isolation and lack of resources fatally determined the kind of warfare the Chinese Nationalists could resort to against the invader. Although the Japanese occupied some more cities south of Canton and drew a little nearer to Chungking by occupying Ichang on the Yangtze in June 1940, by and large the frontline got stabilized along the Peking–Hankow–Canton axis. East of it, along the plains, the superiority of motorized Japanese units, of heavy artillery, and of the aviation excluded all possibility of a Nationalist counter-offensive. Yet west of the line, hilly country and long communication lines rendered all Japanese advance vulnerable to guerilla attacks. Thus, with the Japanese in possession of the economically far more valuable part of the country, a veritable standstill developed. With geography its sole friend, the Nationalist Government had to wait three years until Japan's attack on Pearl Harbour provided it with other allies.

Throughout this undeclared war the Japanese operated through various 'autonomous' régimes in the regions under their control. But once the military situation was more or less stabilized, they returned to their old idea of dealing with occupied China through a Chinese central régime designed to serve their purposes. Their choice fell on Wu Pei-fu, one of the more substantial war-lords, but he finally refused to head the projected puppet government. After that the role was filled by the very Wang Ching-wei who had been a close collaborator of Sun Yat-sen and after his death personified the left wing of the Kuomintang opposed to the break with the Communists.

His government was set up in March 1940 and 'ruled' from Nanking, the old capital. Although a purely artificial creation, Japan pretended to consider his régime as the legal government of China, entered into treaty relations with it, and even assured the puppet régime of her respect of Chinese sovereignty. In order to demonstrate that the Nanking Government was treated as an 'equal', Japan agreed even to the relinquishment of her extra-territorial rights. To complete the fiction, the two governments signed a joint defence pact against Communism and accordingly Japan 'offered' troops to be stationed especially in the northern regions near both the Soviet border and the stronghold of the Chinese Communists. On its part the Nanking régime recognized the fellow-puppet government of Manchukuo and signed even a treaty of alliance with it.

The role of Wang Ching-wei was not unlike that of Marshal Pétain later on in defeated France. He may have been moved by the conviction that after the virtual collapse of China's resistance, his country's best interests would be served by subservience and collaboration. He seems to have believed also that as head of the Nanking régime he might outmanœuvre Japanese intentions. Nevertheless a central government under Wang Ching-wei was a powerful tool in the hands of the Japanese. Wang's prestige, deriving from his long and intimate association with Dr Sun, was not negligible. Although personal ambition and animosity towards Chiang Kai-shek may have powerfully influenced his decision, Wang gathered around him a number of Chinese formerly prominent in the Kuomintang. But Wang Ching-wei and his associates gradually became aware of the futility of their gesture and he died in 1944 a bitter and disillusioned man.

Investment and economic development

In the meantime, as in Manchuria earlier, so now in the rest of China under the Nanking puppet régime, Japanese investments greatly contributed to the development of the country's resources. Either through joint Sino-Japanese undertakings, under purely Japanese companies, or simply through the participation of Japanese skill and capital in Chinese-run enterprises, a number of important economic projects were realized. Factories were built and mines were developed. Railway and bus lines and telegraph networks came to complete the country's rudimentary economic infrastructure. In the great ports dockyards were built or extended and new banks and insurance companies were set up to handle the growing volume of Sino-Japanese exchanges.

This relatively positive side of Japan's presence, however, was amply counter-balanced by other measures of a more openly colonial nature. Perhaps the most irritating for the Chinese was Japan's clumsy control over the educational system. Not only was Japanese made the first foreign language to be taught in the schools but textbooks too were revised so as to serve Japanese ends and, in particular, to spread Japan's propaganda in favour of her 'co-prosperity sphere'. Such and similar measures, together with the generally harsh and condescending attitude of the Japanese in China, tended to annul whatever economic benefits collaboration procured for the Nanking régime. Many Chinese, tired of decades of disorder and disposed to collaborate, were thus alienated and turned once again toward those who continued to resist foreign rule. Moreover, long before the eventual success of indirect Japanese rule could have been measured, the situation was radically modified by international events.

Japanese imperialism unsatisfied

Ever since the collaboration of Japan and Nazi Germany began in 1936, the ambitions of the Japanese imperialists had acquired new dimensions. The defeat of Holland and France in

140

Towards Pearl Harbour

Europe and Great Britain's solitary stand against Germany, left South-east Asia wide open to attack. The temptation was only heightened when, in 1940, Japan signed a mutual aid pact with the apparently victorious Axis powers. And in June 1941, when Hitler invaded the Soviet Union—following a Russo-Japanese neutrality treaty two months earlier—Japan's militarists considered the occasion irresistibly tempting.

Already in September 1940 they began the occupation of Indo-China thus depriving Chiang's régime of even the precarious supply line along the Hanoi–Yunnan railway. Then, profiting by Great Britain's weakened position in the Far East, the Japanese not merely seized every opportunity to lower British prestige but even obtained the closing of the Burma Road, the last artery through which supplies could reach the Chungking régime from the outside world. The only remaining power able to hinder Japan's ambitions in the Pacific theatre was the United States. Although for far too long American economic aid and supplies—particularly petrol and scrap iron —had helped the building up of Japan's war-machine, her limitless ambitions slowly began to swing American public opinion over to the support of Chinese resistance. Relations between Japan and the USA were rapidly deteriorating. Collaboration was giving way to acute tension.

In the eyes of Japan's militarists the hour for the great decision had arrived. Left unexploited it might never return. It was within their reach not merely to bring the whole of China under their control but at the same time to evict the white man from all his possessions from India to the Netherlands East Indies and in the Pacific Ocean. The sole remaining obstacle barring the execution of this grandiose project was America's naval power in the Pacific.

The logical and fatal conclusion was drawn. On 7 December 1941, Japanese planes delivered a surprise attack on Pearl Harbour in Hawaii and dealt a crippling blow to the American fleet. Convinced that America's offensive ability was thus lastingly damaged, the execution began simultaneously of the larger project to replace the white man's power in Asia.

Pearl Harbour

Singapore, Guam and the Philippines were bombed. The International Settlement in Shanghai was occupied and Japanese forces invaded Northern Malaya as a prelude to their conquest of Hong Kong and Singapore, of the Philippines, and of all South-east Asia.

After 8 December 1941, Japan was at war with the United States and Great Britain, as well as with the Netherlands East Indies, Australia and six Latin American countries. All of a sudden China's resistance to Japan's invasion had become part of a far larger whole. And its nature and strategy were soon profoundly affected by it.

After a decade of Japanese aggression, Chiang Kai-shek's prediction came true. China was no longer alone. But who would benefit from the ultimate victory he had foreseen now depended on three factors: on the Kuomintang's ability to conduct China's liberation, on the Communists' tactics to strengthen their position during the war and, finally, on the kind of aid China's new allies, especially the United States, could provide.

The Chungking Régime

IN THE EYES OF MOST CHINESE, in face of Japan's rapid ascendancy, the Nationalist Government was the sole alternative to foreign rule or to the collaborationist subservience of the puppet authorities. Thus, however unwillingly, he found himself leading the country's resistance, at home as abroad, Chiang Kai-shek came to personify China's resistance.

Nothing perhaps could better illustrate this mood than the extraordinary migration of millions of Chinese from coastal China toward the unoccupied interior. Leaving the threatened areas or escaping from the occupied regions, they moved on any available vehicle or simply marched hundreds of miles to reach the provinces under Chungking's rule. Probably the most significant aspect of this great migration was the evacuation of schools and universities from areas invaded by the Japanese. Entire faculties, complete with their professors, students and whatever equipment they could move by lorry or boat, thus transplanted themselves into Szechwan, Yunnan and the other unoccupied provinces. There, under spartan conditions, they gradually resumed their activities. Crowded under inadequate living conditions, finding refuge in old buildings, in temples or in improvised accommodation, China's intelligentsia began its new life. Learning in general being held in high esteem by the Chinese, all this was of great moral support to the Chungking régime.

This amazing manifestation, however, also had other and unexpected results. It brought the urban intellectuals into direct contact with the villages and with the problems of the rural population. Moreover, both the hardships of the journey and the imposed privations of the new surroundings tended to harden the refugee intellectuals. It was an experience that imposed that austere simplicity which, later on, inspired their respect for the ascetic fervour of China's Communists.

Coming from the more developed parts of the country, Spirit of unity

143

understandably, the newcomers did not mix easily with the poorer and more backward local populations. Yet their forced co-existence did not fail to inspire a new spirit of unity and even a sense of common enterprise in face of danger. It also helped to establish contact with some of the hitherto neglected ethnic minorities of the interior and to instil in them a sense of participation as a prelude to their coming emancipation. Above all, the ferment created by this great migration helped to produce constructive enthusiasm which got translated into some positive achievements. Notwithstanding the most adverse circumstances, roads were built, new schools were set up, co-operatives were organized and attempts were made to extend rural credit to help the cultivators. In some cases even some factories were dismantled in the occupied areas and moved in pieces up the Yangtze to be rebuilt in Kuomintang-controlled regions. Small-scale manufacturing was encouraged and an effort was made to explore raw material resources.

The hope existed for a while that misfortune might once again provide the Kuomintang with a chance of renewal. In face of the mortal challenge, patriotism and the instinct of survival were at the disposal of its leaders. Such hopes, however, were soon disappointed.

Military impotence

To begin with, there was the military impotence of the Chungking régime. Committed by the Sian agreement to turn his forces against the Japanese, the Generalissimo lost his best-trained and best-equipped troops during the engagements of the first year following the incident at the Marco Polo bridge. His small air force was all but destroyed. By the time it moved to Chungking, the Nationalist Government was totally deprived of all offensive capability. To be forced on the defensive and to be unable to conceive of any dynamic action against an enemy holding the economically decisive part of the country, was inevitably a demoralizing experience. Perhaps it might have been offset by social and political changes capable of firing the imagination of the masses living under foreign occupation and holding out to them the promise of a better future. But no such changes came from Chungking. If the misty mountains surrounding the new capital had effectively shielded it against the danger of over-land attack by the Japanese, it was also sufficiently removed to cut the government's ties with the masses.

The growing sense of isolation and of static helplessness were further aggravated by the frustrations of the months following America's entry into the war. The Generalissimo and his government greeted the event with an understandable sigh of relief. Henceforth, so they thought, they could lean back and try to prevent the Communists from gaining more power, while the United States and the British Empire would win the war for them.

But contrary to their expectations, the successes of the Japanese during the months following Pearl Harbour were more impressive than ever before. In quick succession they evicted the Americans from the Philippines, and the British and the Dutch from South-east Asia. After Indo-China and Thailand, Burma came under Japanese control and with it the far end of the Burma Road leading to Kunming. After that no other link remained with the outside world than the overland routes from the Soviet Union. But they were long and difficult and Hitler's invasion of Russia seriously reduced the modest flow of supplies which had come along them. So, rather than ease China's plight, the months following the internationalization of the war completed her encirclement and her isolation from her new allies.

Under these circumstances rapid deterioration beset the Chungking régime. Local production was inadequate to offset the effects of the economic blockade. There were shortages, even of essentials. Lack of fuel, of trucks and of spare parts led to a near breakdown of the transport system, affecting even the supply of the fighting forces. The government was unable to control prices and the resulting inflation caused great hardship to all wage earners. This, again, helped to demoralize both the bureaucracy and the intellectuals upon whom the régime particularly depended.

The shift toward the right within the Kuomintang, so noticeable ever since 1927, was now taking on catastrophic dimensions.

Japanese successes

The Nationalist Government needed more revenue, more men for the army and more food to feed them. It tried to finance the war effort by currency inflation. But unable to institute the necessary controls, it got entirely out of hand. To assure essential supplies for the armed forces, grain had to be requisitioned on a large scale. This, in its turn, powerfully reinforced the landlords' influence within both the party and the government. The traditional supporters of the Kuomintang had been the industrial and commercial *bourgeoisie* in the towns and the landlords in the interior. Now most of the big merchants and industrialists were either in Japanese occupied cities or reached the Kuomintang areas ruined and shorn of their influence. Inevitably, then, the landlords, the most reactionary group of the original triumvirate, remained as the main pillar of the Chungking régime. And the conservative pressures which operated on the party became proportionately stronger.

Henceforth land reform was out of the question. Rural conservatism reigned supreme. Even if the Kuomintang apparatus had commanded the required organizational skills, the mounting influence of the landlord class would have prevented the political mobilization of the peasant masses who constituted the overwhelming majority of the population. Although the Kuomintang was responsible for some guerilla activity behind the Japanese lines, it was necessarily limited in view of the ruling circles' understandable reluctance to enlist dynamic popular forces and thus perhaps to endanger their vested interests. The official conviction that in any case the Allies were committed to crush Japan, only helped to encourage this reluctance to mobilize popular energies or the patriotic enthusiasm of the masses.

Under such conditions it is not surprising if corruption, never absent from Kuomintang rule, was beginning to threaten the vitals of the régime like a cancerous growth. The highest dignitaries, including members of the Generalissimo's own family, were turning to profiteering and graft and were amassing fabulous fortunes. Mounting inflation provided them with ample opportunities of currency manipulation and of the hoarding of goods in short supply. While most people had to put up with great hardships and suffered from shortages of even essential goods, members of the government and high officials lived in safety and in comfort, thereby further contributing to the sagging morale of the population as a whole. Inadequately paid and unable to make ends meet, the bureaucracy in its turn was tempted to follow the example of self-seeking given at the top.

The already marked inefficiency of military administration was further aggravated by corrupt fiscal policies in the army. There was the abuse of requisitioning of supplies from the peasantry. Recruiting practices were scandalous and the elementary needs of the soldiers were neglected with appalling cruelty. In the meantime, the ruling clique's passion for illicit profits grew to shameless proportions.

This was well illustrated by the organized smuggling carried on along the Burma Road. At the cost of great sacrifice in life and equipment, the Japanese were expelled from Northern Burma and limited traffic was resumed along the road leading across the border. The goods to be transported needed a special licence. Yet at a time when medical supplies and essential war material were grievously needed, cosmetics and luxury articles of all kinds were transported. They were duly labelled as urgent military supplies and sold at fabulous profit at the other end. All this could not fail to add up to growing demoralization.

In 1944 when US Vice-President Henry A. Wallace was sent to China to see what could be done toward the consolidation of the Chinese war effort, his conversation with the Generalissimo touched frankly upon the poor showing the Chinese troops had made. The Vice-President referred specifically to reports that peasants had been attacking soldiers of the Nationalist armies because they were running away from the Japanese. The Generalissimo made no effort to deny them.

So, the static military situation, unwillingness to rely on popular support, together with widespread corruption and the tendency of the high officials to become a new mandarinate, were rapidly compromising the chances of the Chungking régime. And events beyond the areas under the Nationalists' control did not help to improve the situation.

If Chungking expected quick victory over Japan, by now it had become clear that in the Allies' plans the defeat of the Axis had priority over the Pacific theatre of operations. Nor was Japan slow in profiting from the discomfiture of the Chungking régime. Between 1941 and 1944 she continued to extend the areas she occupied in China in the hope that Chungking would surrender before the United States could rally its forces and provide really effective help. Even if the counter-offensive in the Pacific had begun and American submarines were cutting heavily into the enemy's sea communications, the Japanese established their over-land routes from Korea and Manchuria to South China and to South-east Asia, thus rendering themselves much less vulnerable to America's growing naval supremacy.

At the same time the Japanese were taking a series of astute political measures calculated to flatter Chinese nationalist sentiment and to strengthen political support in the areas under their control. Following similar decisions by the USA and Great Britain in 1943, they turned over to Wang Ching-wei's government their Concessions in five cities, as well as the British Concessions in Canton and Tientsin and the International Settlements in Amoy and Shanghai. They persuaded Italy and Vichy France to follow suit. Italy withdrew from her Concessions in Tientsin and France from Hankow, Canton and Tientsin. The Nanking régime was also given the right to tax Japanese residents, and property taken from Chinese citizens was restored to its rightful owners. Such and similar concessions, though within Japanese controlled territory and under a manifestly puppet régime, did not fail to establish valuable precedents for the future and to some extent at least to strengthen the case of the advocates of collaboration with the Japanese.

Meanwhile, the uneasy collaboration between the Kuomintang and the Communists came under heavy strain. The integration of the Communist armies under Nationalist command was never really realized. From 1941 onward rivalry and suspicion had led to renewed fighting between the two forces. Wishing to see all Chinese energies united against Japan, the Americans noted the renewed dissensions with growing irritation. The fact that Chiang Kai-shek devoted much of his limited resources to the blockade and to the weakening of the Communist armies, and that he even intercepted military and medical supplies sent to the Communist areas by the Americans, merely helped to complicate the already strained relations between the Generalissimo and American representatives in China, most of them already openly sceptical about the Kuomintang's war-effort.

With the Communists steadily extending their influence, and the rivalry for power between them and the Kuomintang going more and more in their favour, there developed inevitable dissensions among the Nationalist Government's followers. In theory the People's Political Council provided a forum for free political discussion. But it had no legislative functions and the freedom of expression the government permitted was strictly limited by its power of intimidation. The minor parties tolerated within the Council—united in the Democratic League—attempted to back American efforts to promote negotiations with the Communists so as to avoid renewed civil war. But they lacked the means and the power to change the course of the events. The Kuomintang was not disposed to tolerate any real opposition and the weapons at its disposal to silence its critics ranged from the secret police and the arbitrary arrest of liberals, to concentration camps and summary executions.

As if to prop up the sagging morale of the Chungking régime, in October 1943 China was given Big Power status as co-signatory of the Moscow Declaration. A month later President Roosevelt and Prime Minister Churchill met Chiang Kai-shek in Cairo and assured him not merely of their support until final victory over Japan, but also of the restitution to China of 'all territories Japan has stolen from the Chinese, such as

Big Power
status

149

Manchuria, Formosa, and the Pescadores' which 'shall be restored to the Republic of China'. During the following months these undertakings were completed by Stalin's promise that the Soviet Union did not intend to support the Chinese Communists and by his undertaking to consider the Nationalists as China's legitimate central government.

But in spite of these assurances and psychological satisfactions, the Chungking régime seemed no longer able to revitalize itself or to escape the strangulation by the self-defeating egotism of its privileged groups. By the end of 1944, when Japan's surrender was within sight, the position of the Nationalist Government was extremely grim. If by then it was probable that the Allies would indeed win the war for China, already it appeared more than doubtful whether the Kuomintang would emerge from it with sufficient prestige and vigour to undertake the country's post-war rehabilitation.

Expansion from Yenan

IF THE CHANGING FORTUNES of the Chinese Communists could be illustrated by a diagram, the dangerous oscillations covering the sixteen years after the foundation of the party would come to a sudden end by the beginning of 1937. From then on, following the Sian incident, the curve would slowly begin to rise and then enter on its steep and uninterrupted ascension till final triumph.

The turning point was clearly Chiang Kai-shek's brief captivity in Sian. It was followed by a series of negotiations and declarations intended to bring about the projected united front. The Communists' final formulation of the compromise was published when the all-out invasion of China began and it was only on 22 September 1937 that the Nationalist Government published the text and thus implicitly legalized both the agreement and the Communist Party.

In exchange for a united front, the Communists promised to abolish the Chinese Soviet Government and to renew their collaboration with the Kuomintang with the aim of enacting a democratic constitution in conformity with Sun Yat-sen's Three Principles. They offered also to place the Red Army under Chiang's authority and declared themselves ready to suspend their policies of land confiscation. The agreement was not formalized by any written alliance. It rested merely upon a series of parallel documents and declarations. But the civil war ceased and in the course of the following months a number of concrete steps were taken to implement the *entente* and to further united resistance against the invader.

The Red Army was reorganized and renamed the Eighth Route Army and came officially under the Government's orders. The Communists' land policies became milder and the Chinese Soviet Government was transformed into a local administration formally dependent on the capital. The Kuomintang made a number of political gestures aiming at the demo-

The Eighth Route Army

151

cratization of public life, including the release of some political prisoners. The Communist forces, by now formally incorporated into the Nationalist armies, received a monetary subsidy as well as a small allotment of ammunition. The Communists were permitted to publish their own newspaper first in Hankow and later in Chungking. Mr Chou En-lai, their principal delegate in the capital, became Vice-Minister of the Political Training Board of the National Military Council, a post he held until 1940. Much later, however, while conducting negotiations in Chungking, he could maintain contacts with diplomats and journalists and was chiefly responsible for the Chinese Communists' picture as 'mere agrarian reformers' so successfully planted in liberal minds all over the world.

But the shadow of the years preceding the 1927 events in Shanghai, lay across the path of genuine compromise and co-operation. There was deep-seated suspicion on both sides. The Communists feared that Chiang would exploit their concession in order to break them, while the Generalissimo was equally convinced that his alliance with the Communists would merely help the extension of their influence. As a result, all concessions were accompanied by compensating measures against double-dealing and, inevitably, collaboration was soon running into serious difficulties.

Rivalry and distrust

After the fall of Hankow in October 1938, already Kuomintang-Communist relations began to deteriorate. Each side accused the other of failing to honour its original engagements and of jockeying for advantages. The Kuomintang claimed that the Communists prevented it from exercising real command over their forces, while the Communists complained of the suppression of their organizations and of the other side's reluctance to respect the zones of influence agreed upon. Though local clashes occurred, the resumption of fighting on a large scale was avoided. But during 1939 the Chungking régime began to enforce a rigid blockade of some of the Communist areas and this resulted in continuous skirmishes. The ensuing, prolonged tension culminated in the so-called 'New Fourth Army Incident' of January 1941.

Expansion from Yenan

The Kuomintang directed the Communist New Fourth Army to move north of the Yangtze and engage the Japanese in the Yellow River area. Its orders being ignored, it attempted to disarm the recalcitrant troops. The Communists maintained that Chungking wished to reduce the areas under their control and intentionally directed their army into a hopeless enterprise. The fighting that resulted was on a large scale and it marked the real beginning of the renewed civil war between the antagonists.

The tension so created lasted throughout the following three years. Although periodically it flared up into open fighting, both sides were determined to settle their differences by negotiation. A long series of declarations and discussions were devoted to the clarification of positions and to the implementation of the various pledges exchanged. These ranged from purely military problems to political ones, involving the question of constitutional government. Yet there was no real progress and the prevailing tension not merely hindered the war-effort against Japan but also threatened the renewal of the civil war. It was under these circumstances that President Roosevelt decided to send his Vice-President to China on a mission of exploration. Mr Henry A. Wallace arrived in Chungking in June 1940 and thus America's direct involvement in China's internal politics began.

If, as it had been stated, the purpose of the Wallace mission was to help consolidate the Chinese war-effort, that foreshadowed America's coming mediation between Kuomintang and Communists. For by then it was obvious that Chinese Communism had grown into a force indispensable not merely in the consolidation of China's resistance, but also in the building of the country's political future.

The progress of the Communists had indeed been spectacular. The aftermath of the Sian incident provided the precarious Yenan base with a welcome breathing space. The losses of the Kuomintang armies during the first year of the Japanese invasion all but removed the mortal, physical threat to the Shansi Soviet. Then, during the period of collaboration with

Spectacular
Communist
progress

the Kuomintang, from July 1937 until the fall of Hankow more than a year later, the Communist Party had grown in strength, had developed its organization, and had steadily extended the area under its control.

During the same period the Communists had tried out their economic and social programme and acquired valuable experience in the art of government. With its university, school of art, military academy and training centre for cadres, Yenan became the laboratory of the political, economic and cultural revolution that the country needed. But perhaps the most significant aspect of the period was that it provided the intelligentsia all over China with an alternative centre of attraction while, visibly, the Kuomintang became prisoner of its most reactionary elements. In fact, from 1937 onward there was a regular pilgrimage of young Chinese with liberal or progressive ideas to what seemed to be the workshop where China's future was shaped.

But confronted by the choice between foreign occupation, the Chungking régime, or Yenan, it is hardly surprising that the Communists exercised much influence over China's youth and on her liberals. The decay of the Chungking régime was in sharp contrast with the Communists' complete certainty in the triumph of their philosophy and in the ultimate victory of their cause. As Confucianism was becoming again the philosophy in power under the Nationalists, the Communists were experimenting with new methods having a wide appeal to the underprivileged majority. While the Kuomintang embarked on the repression of professors and literary men whose liberal influence it wished to extirpate from the universities, the Yenan régime managed to convince the intellectuals that it needed their talents and would assure them the privileges due to their influence and importance. In face of the remoteness and of the military impotence of Chungking, Yenan's propaganda succeeded in depicting the Communists as making the heaviest sacrifices, contributing most effectively to the struggle against Japan, and thus being the real champions of national liberation. Finally, in contrast to the corruption of the Kuomintang, there was the Communists' austerity. Noting the enrichment of Chungking's high officials, people were impressed by the devotion and the self-sacrifice of the Communist leadership.

The impact made by these facts and projections was only underscored by the extent and the nature of the Communists' guerilla activities.

The areas overrun by the Japanese were immense but they were unable permanently to occupy more than the big cities and the main lines of communications. This left vast areas behind the enemy lines almost empty of military power or of any effective administrative control. The policy of the Communists was to infiltrate into these regions and to set up local administrations within them. As time went on, they dispersed the three divisions forming the Eighth Route Army into small guerilla units and, relying on them, substituted themselves for the local authorities. Once so installed behind the Japanese lines, they recruited the local population into new guerilla units and so, gradually, new Communist regions sprang up helping to extend the original Shensi base into Shansi, Hopeh, Shantung and the north of Honan. Later on, the same process was repeated in Central China where they formed the New Fourth Army, the one which provided the cause of the fighting with the Kuomintang forces in 1941. This army too was formed of local recruits with the addition, however, of the scattered remnants of Communist forces which had failed to join the Long March after the evacuation of the Kiangsi Soviet. Thus, the extension of the Communist areas, slow at the beginning, was greatly accelerated after the stabilization of the fronts following the fall of Hankow.

But territorial expansion was only one of the aspects of the Communists' success. The other was in the social and political content of their tactics. Unlike Chungking, the Communists relied upon the organization of the rural masses. The new and more tolerant land policies helped their purpose. The Kiangsi method of the expropriation of landlords now gave way to a more selective process whereby only the absentee landlords' holdings were confiscated while in the case of cultivating

Guerilla activities

Reform and compromise

landowners only rents were controlled by the reduction of the proportion of the crop they exacted from the tenants. Similarly, rather than to abolish debts, interest rates were controlled.

Comparable compromises were made in village self-government. In Kiangsi the poor and landless peasants had formed Soviets. Now, with the exception of absentee landlords, all classes could be elected to the local councils. The new policy was sufficiently effective to offer advantages to the majority, yet mild enough to avoid the kind of revulsion which the Kiangsi excesses had provoked in the threatened classes. These measures were further completed by the redistribution of expropriated land among the landless, by the organization of rural co-operatives, by educational opportunities, and by a larger share given to women in public life.

The new policy of compromise was quickly rewarded by the enthusiasm with which the villagers behind the enemy lines responded to Communist leadership. The result was a guerilla force able to mobilize the energies and the enthusiasm of the villagers and to rely on the dynamic forces of a social upheaval. For the first time in their long history the Chinese masses responded to foreign invasion by a revolutionary resistance able to carry the war behind the enemy lines. Liberation was thus acquiring a double meaning for them. While it promised the recovery of the country's independence, it implied also the simultaneous freeing of the masses from the oppression of landlords, from that of the bureaucracy and of the capitalists, all conveniently covered by the spacious epithet of imperialist exploiters.

The spread of Communism

The communication lines and the cities held by the Japanese were thus harassed by Communist guerillas. How effective such attacks were militarily, or whether they caused much more inconvenience to the Japanese than Chungking's military operations, may be open to debate. But the Communists' guerilla warfare aimed at more than mere military results. It helped both to spread their control over resources and local administration, and to forge the Communist Party's ties with the peasantry.

By the end of 1944, when the morale of the Chungking régime was at its lowest ebb, the Communist-controlled areas had spread all over North China, through several regions in Central China, and down to isolated islands of influence even in the south of the country.

From one million after the Long March, the number of people living under Communist rule had grown to a hundred million. The original Shensi army of 30,000 men in 1935 developed into a force of one million, composed mainly of peasants, and supported by a militia of nearly twice that size. As for the Chinese Communist Party itself, notwithstanding deviations and internal struggles, its membership rose from barely fifty thousand in 1937 to over a million in 1945. By then it was the largest in the world outside the Soviet Union.

As Chungking's prestige continued to decline, a proportionate growth took place in the Communists' political self-confidence. By far the weaker in 1937, six years later they were no longer in a mood to offer concessions to the Kuomintang. And to fit the new situation, a doctrine was being evolved to bring official party theory up to date.

In 1940 Mao Tse-tung published his celebrated essay *On New Democracy*, claimed to be a significant addition to Marxist-Leninist theory. Written in his clear, vigorous and easily accessible style, it set out to prove that the current phase of the Chinese Revolution ought to be led by the 'joint dictatorship of several revolutionary classes'. At that stage already it voiced the Communists' confidence that they could claim the leadership of such a 'joint dictatorship'. Indirectly it also implied that the 'united front', based on Kuomintang supremacy, had for the Communists no further utility. In the course of the following three years the situation continued to develop to the detriment of Chungking and by 1944 Yenan was calling for a coalition. Mao's answer to the Kuomintang's refusal was, in April 1945, another political document, entitled *On Coalition Government*.

The principles advanced in the *New Democracy* were now spelled out in greater detail and assorted with concrete demands

Mao Tse-tung on 'New Democracy'

on the Kuomintang. Mao Tse-tung called for a coalition of classes from which only the landlords, the 'bureaucratic capitalists', and collaborators with the Japanese would be excluded. In contrast, even the small landowners and the 'national capitalists' were to be admitted to the broad national front. Finally, to allay the fears of the middle class, Mao explained that the dictatorship the Communists called for was not that of the Communist Party or of the 'proletariat', but that of the 'people'. And the distinction, set out in detail, was not negligible in helping to deprive the Kuomintang of part at least of its all-important middle-class support.

So, with the rivalry for post-war supremacy going more and more in favour of Yenan, nothing but mutual concessions and the resumption of negotiations could offer any hope of averting renewed civil war. To bring them about had for some time been the growing preoccupation of the most directly involved ally of China—the United States.

American Involvement

AMERICA'S ATTITUDE OF COMPROMISE in 1931 in face of Japan's aggression in Manchuria was not basically modified when, six years later, the Japanese army began the invasion of the rest of China. There was public revulsion against involvement in war. Also American business interests at home or in China were not anti-Japanese. Japan was proving herself a far better customer than China ever was, trade in petrol and scrap iron was highly profitable and, in any case, Japan stood for 'law and order' in face of the mobs incited by Chinese nationalists.

But the revelation of Japan's limitless ambitions, followed by military successes menacing all western positions in Asia, were beginning to impress public opinion. The bombing of some American vessels on the Yangtze in December 1937, and the news of Japanese atrocities in Nanking and elsewhere, were slowly transforming apathy into anger and hostility.

American policy toward China was traditionally a compromise between the views of business men, government officials, and of missionaries. Of the three, the missionaries were by far the most vocal and the most influential. By now they were staunch allies of the Kuomintang, and Chiang Kai-shek—a convert to Methodism and reported to participate in daily Bible readings—was not merely their idol but also the symbol of a China victimized by the Japanese. This enthusiasm, most effectively communicated to the American public, powerfully influenced American opinion and helped the Government to effect the modifications in its policy dictated by the general world situation. Missionary influence

In July 1938 a 'moral embargo' was placed on the export of planes to Japan and a year later its scope was broadened so as to include also petrol used in aeroplanes. The commercial treaty with Japan was denounced and once it lapsed the export to Japan of a number of commodities was banned, including petroleum products and scrap iron. In the meantime, released from the restrictions on its naval armaments imposed by the Washington Treaty, the USA began to enlarge its navy and, from 1940 onward, to construct air and submarine bases in the Pacific area. Simultaneously, American political and military advisers were placed at the disposal of the Chinese Government.

Throughout 1940 relations between the two countries were deteriorating fast. The economic measures decided by Washington were causing anxiety in Japan and negotiations were undertaken against a background of mounting tension. Washington made it clear, however, that no return to normal trade relations would be possible before Japan changed her policies, abandoned her aggression, and entered a new collective security system in the Far East. Unwilling to abandon their chosen course or to let pass their tempting opportunities, Japan's rulers riposted with the attack on Pearl Harbour.

Air-lift to China

But by the time the United States and the British Commonwealth had thus become allies of China, their means to extend effective aid to her were severely limited. Great Britain was fully occupied with the protection of her own direct interests. The USA was ill-prepared for the war forced upon her. Moreover, Japan controlled most of the Pacific coast and all the Chinese ports. Though Lend-Lease aid, inaugurated before Pearl Harbour, was stepped up after America's entry into the war, the difficulties of access maintained it at a relatively modest volume. Four months after Pearl Harbour the road from Burma was sealed off. The overland route from the USSR apart, only the slender air-lift from India remained. Flown by Chinese and American pilots, it was one of the most difficult and most vulnerable supply operations of the Second World War. Subject to attack by Japanese planes from Burma, it flew over the tremendous mountain barrier between India and China. Yet its symbolic importance apart, as China's last link with the outside world, eventually it transported more cargo and soldiers into China than had ever passed along the Burma Road.

In the meantime, the US Fourteenth Air Force, under General Chennault, rendered useful services to the Nationalist régime, practically defenceless against Japan's air force. Financially, the United States voted a $500 million loan to China in early 1942. In the same year, both America and Great Britain unilaterally renounced for the future all their remaining special privileges in China. This was followed by another good-will gesture in 1943. The US Congress repealed the Chinese Exclusion Laws and by so admitting Chinese immigrants, it removed a long-standing irritant in Sino-American relations.

All this, of course, did not amount to the decisive aid Chiang Kai-shek had foreseen once war with Japan would be internationalized. Although the amount of equipment put at the disposal of the Chinese was substantial and the number of advisers, military and civilian, steadily increased, Allied commitments in other theatres of the war, and the physical obstacles to delivery in particular, made it inevitable that the Chungking authorities would be disappointed. Their effort to secure that victory over Japan should have priority over the defeat of the Axis, was unsuccessful. Moreover, more and more American strategic thinking evolved toward direct attack from the Pacific islands, rather than in favour of a long and costly campaign across China to be followed by additional naval operations aiming at the invasion of Japan from the mainland. Under these circumstances the major interest of the Allies was to maintain Chinese resistance against the invader until either through South-east Asia or through the liberated Chinese ports large-scale aid could be provided. By implication this meant Allied concern both for the fighting morale of the Chinese armies and for the co-ordination of their war effort, irrespective of their ideological allegiance. It is there that America's political difficulties in China began in earnest.

No decisive aid

As American forces in China increased, both officers and men had ample opportunities to familiarize themselves with prevailing conditions under the Chungking régime as well as in other parts of the country, including those under Communist rule. They, as much as the American diplomatic representatives in China, noted the corruption and the repressive nature of the Generalissimo's régime. In contrast, many among them became aware that the Communists were carrying out reforms and were harvesting in exchange the support of the masses. All this was accompanied by growing friction between Chinese and Americans, due partly to the alleged condescension of some American personnel, and partly to the criticism they had voiced against the Chungking régime. In any case, American personnel in China had been watching with growing irritation how both Nationalists and Communists had been trying to conserve their strength to fight it out after the United States had crushed Japan for them.

Impatience with Chungking

In the words of Mr Dean Acheson's covering letter to the American White Paper on *United States Relations with China*—published in August 1949—'The reports of United States military and diplomatic officers reveal a growing conviction through 1943 and 1944 that the Government and the Kuomintang had apparently lost the crusading spirit that won them the people's loyalty during the early years of the war. In the opinion of many observers they had sunk into corruption, into a scramble for place and power, and into reliance on the United States to win the war for them and to preserve their own domestic supremacy. . . . These observers were already fearful in 1943 and 1944 that the National Government might be so isolating itself from the people that in the post-war competition for power it would prove itself impotent to maintain its authority. . . .'

Washington's growing concern prompted the mission of Vice-President Wallace in June 1944. He was to explore the situation and appraise the chances of *rapprochement* between Kuomintang and Communists. Though Chiang Kai-shek assured him that he desired 'a political solution' to the conflict with the Communists, the effective prosecution of the war was not much advanced. It was estimated at the time that some 300,000 of the Government's best troops were diverted to watch the Communists. Yet in spite of the frequent military friction between the Kuomintang and the Communist armies, both sides pretended to seek a negotiated settlement. In fact, though interrupted by periodic clashes, the negotiations had never ceased since 1941.

But renewed Japanese military successes convinced President Roosevelt of the need for urgent action and he made the suggestion to Chiang that an American General be appointed to the command of all Chinese and American forces in China, though under the Generalissimo's authority. He put forward the name of General Stilwell for the role.

This attempt to co-ordinate and to direct the Chinese war-effort, first accepted in principle by Chiang, got shipwrecked on his unwillingness to yield effective command. Stilwell, in the Far East since 1942, was no admirer of the Generalissimo and relations between the two men reached a point where he had to be recalled to Washington and be replaced by Major-General Wedemeyer. A month before leaving China, Stilwell sent Washington his plain-spoken appraisal of the situation: '. . . Chiang Kai-shek has no intention of making further efforts to prosecute the war. Anyone who crowds him towards such action will be blocked or eliminated . . . [he] believes he can go on milking the United States for money and munitions by using the old gag about quitting if he is not supported. He believes the war in the Pacific is nearly over, and that by delaying tactics, he can throw the entire burden on us. He has no intention of instituting any real democratic régime or of forming a united front with the Communists. He himself is the main obstacle to the unification of China and her co-operation in a real effort against Japan. . . . I am now convinced that, for the reasons stated, the United States will not get any real co-operation from China while Chiang Kai-shek is in power. I believe he will only continue his policy and delay, while grabbing for loans and post-war aid, for the purpose of maintaining his present position, based on one-party government, a reactionary policy, or the suppression of democratic ideas with the active aid of his gestapo.'

In his final report to the War Department, General Stilwell's conclusions were even more explicit: '. . . We could gain little

General
Stilwell's
appraisal

163

by supporting the attitude of the Chiang régime. We could have gained much by exerting pressure on Chiang to co-operate and achieve national unity, and if proved unable to do this, then in supporting those elements in China which gave promise of such development.'

The American dilemma   This harsh judgment may have been the view of a soldier preoccupied above all with the efficient prosecution of the war. But the hint contained in his summing up touched upon the crucial problem in the centre of all discussion among the makers of America's Far Eastern policy, as well as in the complex, triangular negotiations going on between Americans and the representatives of both Chungking and Yenan.

The unenviable dilemma of the Americans emerged clearly from the despatches sent to Washington by Foreign Service Officers toward the end of 1944. 'If the Generalissimo neither precipitates a civil war nor reaches an understanding with the Communists, he is still confronted with defeat,' said one of them. 'Chiang's feudal China cannot long co-exist alongside a modern dynamic popular government in North China. The Communists are in China to stay. And China's destiny is not Chiang's but theirs. . . . In this unhappy dilemma, the United States should attempt to prevent the disaster of civil war through adjustment of the new alignment of power in China by peaceful processes. The desirable means to this end is to encourage the reform and revitalization of the Kuomintang so that it may survive as a significant force in a coalition government. . . .'

'We should not now abandon Chiang Kai-shek,' said another despatch, also in November 1944. 'To do so at this juncture would be to lose more than we could gain. . . . But we must be realistic. We must not indefinitely underwrite a politically bankrupt régime. And, if the Russians are going to enter the Pacific War, we must make a determined effort to capture politically the Chinese Communists rather than to allow them to go by default wholly to the Russians. Furthermore, we must fully understand that by reason of our recognition of the Chiang Kai-shek Government as now constituted we are committed to

164

a steadily decaying régime and severely restricted in working out military and political co-operation with the Chinese Communists. A coalition Chinese Government in which the Chinese Communists find a satisfactory place is the solution of this impasse most desirable to us. It provides our greatest assurance of a strong, united, democratic, independent and friendly China —our basic strategic aim in Asia and the Pacific. . . . If the Russians enter North China and Manchuria, we obviously cannot hope to win the Communists entirely over to us, but we can through control of supplies and post-war aid expect to exert considerable influence in the direction of Chinese nationalism and independence from Soviet control. . . .'

Such and similar considerations may have moved President Roosevelt to determine and to limit Russia's role once she honoured the promise made at the Teheran Conference to enter the war against Japan within two or three months after Germany's defeat. At the beginning of 1945 no one knew whether or when the atomic bomb would become operational. The Japanese Kwantung Army in Manchuria was intact and formidable. Military opinion was that Japan would have to be defeated primarily on the land, in China and Japan, and that the direct invasion of her shores would be an operation very costly in Allied and particularly American lives. To induce Russia to enter the war, therefore, was both to shorten it and to reduce US losses. That undertaking was obtained at Teheran. The bill for it was presented in February 1945 at Yalta.

Previously, in August 1944, General Hurley, the American President's special representative in China, met Mr Molotov in Moscow. On that occasion Molotov disclaimed any Russian intention to support China's Communists. In fact, he spoke about them in rather condescending terms. He stated that the Soviet Union would be content if the Americans aided the Chinese in the unification of their country and in their war-effort and that the USSR had no objection to America 'taking the lead economically, politically and militarily in Chinese affairs'.

Russia enters the Japanese war

The Chinese Revolution

Yalta Six months later, at Yalta, in addition to the restoration of all Russian territories taken by Japan after her victory in 1905, Stalin also demanded that the Soviet Union be restored to her pre-1905 position in Manchuria (over which, however, Chinese sovereignty would be recognized), and that 'the *status quo* in Outer-Mongolia shall be preserved'. In exchange, the USSR would conclude an alliance with the Nationalist Government 'in order to render assistance to China with its armed forces for the purpose of liberating China from the Japanese yoke'.

China was not present at Yalta. Nor, in view of security considerations, could Chungking immediately be informed of the terms of the agreement. Roosevelt and Churchill stipulated, however, that the Generalissimo's agreement would be needed concerning the provisions relating to Outer Mongolia, Port Arthur and Dairen, and to the Manchurian railways.

These arrangements, much contested after the unforeseeable turn of the military situation in the Allies' favour, have been justified on several grounds. Once Russia's entry into the war was accepted as of vital military importance, it was preferable to define her recompense rather than to let her take it without agreed limits. Russia's claim for access to ice-free ports in the Far East appeared justified. Then, the Soviet Union was brought into the emerging international organization of the post-war world also in the Far East. Last but not least, Russia undertook to give her moral and military support to the Nationalist Government and to it alone.

In May 1945 these premises were reiterated when Harry Hopkins, the US Ambassador in Moscow, met Stalin. He once again expressed his conviction that Chiang Kai-shek was better qualified to undertake the unification of China than were the Chinese Communists, that America would have to play a leading role in China's post-war reconstruction, and that he would welcome Chinese participation in the rebuilding of Manchuria's administration. All this helped to support the prevailing impression that Stalin preferred a weak and disunited Chinese neighbour and that he neither desired the Communists' arrival to power nor considered them ready.

166

American Involvement

On June 4, President Truman informed T. V. Soong, brother-in-law of Chiang Kai-shek and both Premier and Foreign Minister, about Stalin's views. Next day, General Hurley, the American Ambassador in Chungking, disclosed to the Generalissimo the terms of the Yalta agreement. Although resented, at least officially, the failure to consult China beforehand was accepted without undue complications and negotiations with Russia began forthwith. On 14 August 1945, the Sino-Soviet Treaty of Alliance—to last for thirty years—was signed.

Eight days earlier an atomic bomb exploded over the city of Hiroshima and another destroyed the city of Nagasaki two days later. The same day, on August 8, Russian troops entered Manchuria. And at noon, the day after the Sino-Soviet Treaty was signed, the Emperor of Japan's broadcast announced his country's surrender.

The international position of Chiang Kai-shek had never been stronger. The enemy that had made war on China for fourteen years was crushed. The Soviet Union recognized his régime as the central government of China and agreed 'not to take part in any coalition whatever' directed against it. China was officially recognized as one of the five powers with a permanent seat on the Security Council. And the Generalissimo became one of the Big Five arbiters of the post-war world's fate.

The question that remained to be answered was whether he could establish within China the authority that would be proportionate to the role the outside world had accorded to him in advance.

Post-War Search for Compromise

WHILE RUSSIAN TROOPS were pouring into Manchuria, the race began for the reoccupation of the areas formerly under Japanese control. The fear of the Nationalist Government was that Communist army units might take over regions where they faced the Japanese and that by disarming them they might come into possession of their equipment. But due mainly to the logistic aid of the Americans, transporting Chiang's troops by sea and by air, the race was won by the Nationalists.

The critical area was Manchuria. The Kuomintang was afraid that the Soviet commanders there might collaborate with the Communist guerillas and so bar the entry of the Nationalist troops. The economic importance of Manchuria made it decisive for post-war reconstruction. Thanks to Japan's investments and technicians, Manchuria alone had four times more industries than the rest of China. Its agricultural surpluses were sorely needed to alleviate shortages in the rest of the country. Yet an American air-lift, much resented by Yenan, enabled the Nationalists to occupy the principal centres of Manchuria and thus to upset Communist hopes of gaining control of this vital area.

But not since 1911 had any central government effectively controlled Manchuria. To bring it now under the Nationalists' rule led inevitably to serious difficulties. These were only aggravated by Russia's ambiguous attitude, the result of a compromise between her obligation to support the Nationalist Government and her fear lest it should become too strong with American backing.

Soviet equivocation To begin with, Russia declared legitimate 'war booty' all industrial equipment that had helped Japan's war-effort. She began to dismantle and to remove considerable quantities. Emerging from the devastation of Hitler's invasion, such equipment, no doubt, was urgently needed in the Soviet Union. But by crippling Manchuria's mines and factories, it meant also

168

a blow to the Kuomintang's economic hopes. Yet simultaneously, in conformity with their treaty obligations, the Russians collaborated with the Nationalist authorities and helped them to reoccupy the urban centres of Manchuria. As for the countryside, it was penetrated mainly by the Communists' forces. But the equivocal attitude of the Soviet authorities soon led to another complication. Once the Russians had completed the disarmament of the Japanese troops in Manchuria and were beginning to withdraw the bulk of their forces, they arranged to store large quantities of Japanese arms and ammunition in such a way that, without much difficulty, the Communists could take possession of them. For the first time the Chinese Communists thus acquired modern weapons and this, so it would seem, was the only material help they ever received from the Soviet Union throughout their long struggle for power.

In the meantime, the Generalissimo's government returned to its former capital of Nanking. It recovered the main cities and all the Yangtze valley. Soon it controlled more of China than even at the height of the Kuomintang's successes after the Northern Expedition. But the problems the government had to face were immense. Eight years of war left in its wake devastation, disorganization and much physical suffering. This was further aggravated by the masses' understandable impatience for rapid and effective measures to improve their material condition. Production was below pre-war levels while the number of consumers had grown. Transportation systems were badly run down and the railways were short of both locomotives and rolling-stock. Disorganization was such that even available supplies and foreign aid could not be applied where needs were most urgent. Only a strong, selfless and highly efficient government would have been able to face problems of such gravity and magnitude.

It soon became clear that the Kuomintang emerged from the war without any such qualities. The liberal elements within it were eclipsed and the most reactionary interests controlled the party machine. Returning to the big cities from their years of

Kuomintang failure

169

exile in the interior, the major preoccupation of its officials appeared to be to make up for lost opportunities. To get rich quickly was the supreme goal and no refinement of corrupt practices was neglected. The levity, the arrogance and the irresponsibility of most of the high dignitaries rapidly convinced the people that they could expect no improvement from the Nanking Government. The landlords were given a free hand to step up at will their oppression and their exploitation of the villagers. Mounting inflation continued to procure fortunes for speculators and hoarders, while it brought ruin to the small people who depended on fixed incomes. And in place of new ideas, there was the aridity of Confucian platitudes. No wonder, then, if the liberals, the intellectuals and young people in general were turning in disillusionment toward the Communists, seeing in them the only remaining alternative.

Presiding over this depressing performance, Chiang Kai-shek relied on his prefabricated prestige as one of the victorious war leaders; on the support of financial and business interests; on his control of the cities, railways and the industries; as well as on his armies and on the terror of his secret police.

But it became clear fairly soon how unreal the situation was. While formally and legally all China was governed by Nanking, there was in fact a rival government. It not merely challenged the Kuomintang régime's authority, but it also controlled large areas and commanded the sympathies if not the allegiance of millions living beyond them.

If such a situation eminently suited Russia's purposes, this was not the case with the Americans. Global tension between the USA and the USSR was growing and the Nationalist-controlled and internationally recognized Chinese Government was too vulnerable to fill the strategic vacuum between the United States and the Soviet Union.

American
mediation

Under these circumstances the Americans had to choose between three alternatives. To acquiesce in the Chinese Communists' rise to power, was unthinkable. To ensure the extension of the Kuomintang Government's power over all China would have required direct and large-scale military intervention, unacceptable to American public opinion. The remaining alternative was continued mediation between Kuomintang and Communists. True, if unsuccessful, it was to imply unilateral interference and that, in view of the Kuomintang's morale and Chiang's inability to change it, on the losing side. But if successful, it promised a coalition and thus a united and stable China outside either the American or the Soviet strategic zone.

The report of the Commanding General of the China theatre, in November 1945, rendered the choice of this third alternative inevitable. While castigating the Nationalists' corruption and lack of reforms, General Wedemeyer told Washington that Chiang would be incapable of occupying Manchuria and that he would be unable to consolidate his position even in North China unless he first reached a satisfactory settlement with the Communists. Yet, being sceptical of the chances of such a settlement, he recommended recourse to foreign administrators and technicians, as well as to a joint trusteeship over Manchuria by the USA, Great Britain and the Soviet Union, until Nanking could assume control.

It was against this background that, by the end of November, President Truman decided to send to China his former Chief of Staff General George C. Marshall with instructions to assist in the 'unification of China by peaceful, democratic methods'. His mission lasted for just over a year and it was America's last major effort of political bridge-building in post-war China.

Right after the war the impression may have seemed justified that the Communists were ready for a negotiated compromise. At Chiang Kai-shek's invitation (and with the American Ambassador guaranteeing his personal safety), Mao Tse-tung himself had gone to Chungking. The negotiations had lasted for six weeks. When, on October 10, a joint statement was issued, the concessions agreed to provoked violent criticism in the Communist ranks in Yenan. In exchange for what seemed to be substantial concessions, Mao obtained nothing but vague promises. Very soon, indeed, the Kuomintang renewed its military operations and this was interpreted by the Communists as a clear breach of Chiang's undertaking to seek settlement by

General
Marshall's
mission

The Chinese Revolution

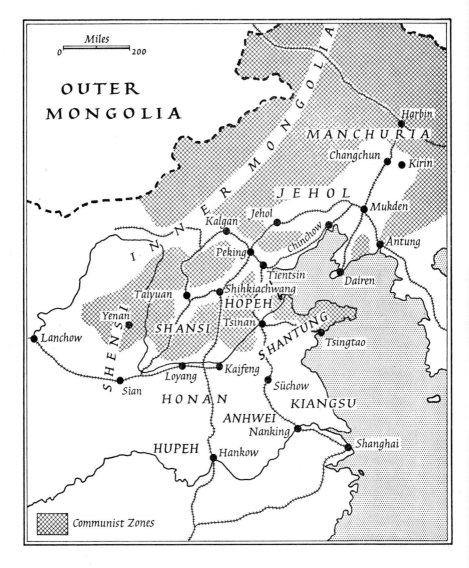

The Civil War 1945–1949
The military situation at the beginning of 1947

peaceful means only. Whether by the time General Marshall arrived in China either of the two partners still wished for a compromise, is uncertain. Probably both the Kuomintang and the Communists wanted to gain time to improve their positions and to avoid large-scale civil war and neither of them wished to give the impression that it had refused to negotiate. However, General Marshall's prestige, tact and patience soon appeared to yield results.

His aims were three-fold. In the first place, he wanted a lasting cease-fire; he wished to bring about gradual military and political reconciliation; and he hoped that the democratization of the Kuomintang Government and the mediation of the minor parties would further a negotiated settlement.

In fact a truce was concluded in January 1946 and a tripartite committee (with American participation) was to supervise its enforcement. The Generalissimo announced that the National Government would grant certain fundamental democratic rights and some efforts were made to bring into being an assembly (the Political Consultative Conference) in which next to the Kuomintang, the Communists as well as the small political parties would be represented. The Communists even consented to the movement of Nationalist troops into Manchuria and there was agreement in principle both on the reciprocal reduction of armed forces and on their gradual integration into units with mixed contingents.

But the hopeful beginning was soon followed by disappointment. In April fighting broke out again. Whatever importance could be attached to the Communists' verbal agreement to political co-operation, it had become clear that, even under strong American pressure, Chiang Kai-shek was unwilling to have the Kuomintang one-party control substantially modified. As for the 'minor parties', they revealed themselves insignificant, with no more than limited and vague influence in some academic circles, and certainly too ineffectual to influence in any way the relationship of the two major antagonists.

With admirable patience, General Marshall persevered in his attempt to paper over the cracks. There were renewed, long

An impossible task

and tortuous negotiations. All the old ground was gone over again and again. Week after week each side kept trying to shift responsibility to the other and politely to oblige the illustrious mediator. Finally, General Marshall asked for his recall.

He left China on 8 January 1947. In his final report he blamed his failure on the extremists on both sides. Then, assuming his new office as Secretary of State, he continued to exert his influence in order to further the aims he had been working for during his mission.

While failing to respond to the Secretary of State's call for reforms and the democratization of his régime, Chiang Kai-shek persisted in his obsession of annihilating the military might of the Communists. When, on the eve of his departure, General Marshall had warned the Generalissimo of the inflationary consequences of futile military operations, Chiang had assured him that the Communist forces would be 'exterminated' within a few months. Now, in the spring of 1947, he was determined to prove his point and he resumed his 'annihilation campaigns'.

The Kuomintang offensive

The Kuomintang appeared to strengthen its military positions in Manchuria. Much of the area in Central China, which the Communists had held only lightly, was reoccupied. Other armies advanced toward the North-west and on March 19 occupied Yenan itself. The symbolic importance of the fall of the Communist capital was duly exploited by official propaganda and was utilized in an attempt to impress foreign opinion. That the victory was illusory as the Communists had evacuated the region well in advance, was not mentioned. Nor was it revealed that pursuing their traditional, resilient tactics the Communists maintained their armies intact while the Nationalists' communication lines grew steadily longer and more vulnerable to guerilla attacks.

Clearly, the official satisfaction of the Kuomintang showed little regard for the realities of the situation. Superficially, the Nationalist military successes may have seemed impressive. Yet the general situation was rapidly deteriorating.

Since the end of the war China had been receiving substantial economic aid from the western powers, from international organizations, and from the United States in particular. The value of goods delivered by UNRRA (United Nations Relief and Rehabilitation Administration) alone was nearly $700 million. Aid worth several times more had come from the Americans in the form of transport, services, civilian and military supplies, and loans. In fact US grants and credits to the Nationalist Government merely since the surrender of Japan amounted to about $2,000 million. But reckless expenditure on military operations continued to absorb over two-thirds of the budget. The most spectacular inflation known in history was transforming the routine of daily existence into a nightmare of handling stacks of banknotes valueless overnight. And while the material conditions of the masses were thus becoming intolerable, the spiritual bankruptcy of the régime was leading to complete psychological dependence upon foreign aid. Corruption, the activities of the secret police, and administrative inefficiency were creating an unbridgeable gap between people and government. There were widespread student demonstrations and their bloody repression aroused public indignation. There was alarming evidence of the Kuomintang troops' fast sinking morale and reports became frequent of soldiers selling their arms to the Communists and even of entire units surrendering to them, won over by their propaganda.

Alarmed by these developments, in July 1947 President Truman despatched General Wedemeyer on a fact-finding mission to China. A month later, when his tour of investigation was completed, he issued a blunt statement: 'To regain and maintain the confidence of the people'—he said in his summing up—'the Central Government will have to effect immediately drastic, far-reaching political and economic reforms. Promises will no longer suffice. Performance is absolutely necessary. It should be accepted that military force in itself will not eliminate communism.' In addition, and in view of the Nationalists' untenable position in the North, General Wedemeyer also recommended that the United Nations should bring about a truce in Manchuria and put the region under joint Chinese, Soviet, British, French and American guardianship.

America calls for reforms

175

General Wedemeyer's public strictures were aimed to bring home to the Nationalist Government that the United States were unwilling to continue their unconditional moral and material support without a corresponding effort on the part of their Chinese protégés to put their house in order.

To stave off such a definite reappraisal of Washington's policy, Chiang Kai-shek and the Kuomintang leaders thought it advisable to give the impression that they would broaden their régime's popular basis. The period of political tutelage under the Kuomintang was coming to its end, they declared, and the time had come to proceed toward the next stage foreseen by Sun Yat-sen, a democratic multi-party system. Accordingly, a National Assembly was convened in Nanking, called upon to adopt a new constitution. Though neither the Communists nor most of the 'minor parties' could be induced to participate, the Kuomintang went ahead with its unconvincing experiment. In March 1948 the National Assembly's meeting produced no greater result than the election of the President and the Vice-President of the Republic.

Too little and too late

Insisting first that he would decline it, Chiang Kai-shek finally accepted his election to the Presidential office. As for the Vice-President, there was genuine competition and, at the end, Li Tsung-jen, a candidate strongly opposed by the Generalissimo, was elected. A former war-lord in Kiangsi, Li was by now identified with the relatively liberal elements within the Kuomintang and his election seemed symptomatic of the growing disillusionment with the Generalissimo's leadership. But the half-hearted gestures aiming at liberalization deceived no one. They were too little and far too late.

In any case Chiang's position within the party was still unassailable. Moreover neither his methods nor his way of thinking had changed. His stubborn pride and his fatal loyalty to even the most corrupt and most incompetent of his collaborators or members of his family, maintained him in a grandiose but catastrophic attachment to self-defeating methods. Unquestionably sincere and courageous, Chiang was temperamentally incapable of understanding the real source of Com-

176

munist strength. To him reforms were concessions to American insistence rather than means to gain popular support. Right, perhaps, in persisting in his faith that China needed strong and authoritarian government, he was certainly wrong in overlooking the decisive importance of the social and economic content of the paternalism he stood for. As for the Americans in China, they were welded to Chiang in irritated but helpless solidarity. Really effective sanctions to propel him toward reforms immediately provoked vehement accusations of treason on behalf of the Generalissimo's numerous and influential admirers in the United States. Meanwhile in China, there was no one within sight to perform his task with greater promise of success.

So, during these months of impending doom, while clear-sighted analyses of the situation were not lacking, nothing happened capable of changing the depressing course of events. Clearly, the time for negotiations was over. The leaders of the Kuomintang could not believe that the Americans would be unable or unwilling to save them. The Americans, on their part, had faith in democracy and in the miracle that the Kuomintang could or would apply it. In the meantime, the Communists were marshalling their forces probably unaware that their triumph was so near. And the Generalissimo, little affected by the events, informed the National Assembly in May 1948 that he hoped to annihilate the Communists within three months.

The beginning of the end

But before the Assembly's session was over, the tide had suddenly begun to turn. This time, however, it was soon clear that instead of just another phase in the shifting civil war, this was the unexpected beginning of the last scene of the last act.

The Finale

By the end of 1948 there were probably few Chinese left who still hoped that reforms would make their government more honest, more competent, or less cruelly oppressive. Those who still believed that it could beat the Communists must have been even more rare. Though repeatedly advised to cut his losses and withdraw his armies from Manchuria, Chiang Kai-shek dispersed his troops over an area far surpassing his means. The over-extended communication lines were highly vulnerable to guerilla attacks. The fighting morale of the troops was in rapid decline. Communist guerillas blockaded the cities, cut supplies and disastrously accentuated the economic chaos resulting from extravagant military expenditure. And notwithstanding an abortive currency reform in the summer of 1948, inflation was growing again to fantastic proportions.

The Kuomintang's shortcomings were the greatest assets to the Communists' propaganda. By now it was also violently anti-American. It accused the United States of supporting the Kuomintang against the people and of prolonging the civil war. Less in need of the support of all classes than during the anti-Japanese war, the Communists were returning to a more radical land redistribution programme and this helped to mobilize behind them the peasant masses wherever their occupation extended. And Mao Tse-tung's programme of 'coalition' tended to reconcile all the hesitants who had lost faith in the Nationalists.

The fall of Manchuria

As was to be expected, the collapse began in Manchuria. Since the beginning of 1948 the major Nationalist garrisons, containing the government's best armies, had been isolated. While scoring some spectacular victories in Central China, involving the surrender of large numbers of troops, by October the Communist nutcracker closed in on Manchuria. Mukden and the other big cities surrendered or were taken in quick succession. The best American-trained and equipped units of the Nationalist armies disintegrated or went over with all their equipment intact.

But after the fall of Manchuria the tempo of the civil war only accelerated. Marching down from Mukden, the Communist armies won one of the decisive contests of modern Chinese history, the three weeks' battle of Hsuchow. There, the flower of the Kuomintang armies were either destroyed or entire divisions defected, once again handing over their guns and other equipment. Beyond Hsuchow, the cutting edge of the Communist offensive was fast tearing to shreds whatever armed resistance remained. Tientsin fell on 15 January 1949, and a week later Peking surrendered without resistance. By the end of January, the Communist armies arrived on the Yangtze.

It had been estimated that during the four and a half months, from the beginning of the Manchurian collapse to the occupation of Peking, the Nationalist armies had lost over a million men. Most of them defected to the Communists, taking with them over half a million rifles and huge quantities of other modern equipment, most of it American. The Communists were thus acquiring even American planes, as well as small naval units and a cruiser which had been transferred by Great Britain to the Nationalist Government. If the Nationalists began 1948 with a three-to-one superiority in combat forces, by the time Peking surrendered and the Communist forces were reorganized, they had achieved slight numerical superiority.

Flushed with success and with complete victory within sight, there was a significant shift in Communist propaganda. It now switched to a call for the restoration of peace. The Communists, so the argument ran, desired peace and those who were opposed served the interests of foreign imperialists. Inevitably, this was highly effective and even within the Kuomintang there were voices urging a negotiated settlement. The most prominent spokesman of peace negotiations was Li Tsung-jen, the Vice-President himself.

With inspired rumours in circulation about Chiang Kai-shek's eventual retirement, the Nationalist Government was

Chiang
Kai-shek
retires

179

making desperate attempts to obtain American promises of further large-scale aid or of other guarantees to halt the Communists north of the Yangtze. But the situation was such that only the intervention of American armed forces on a large scale would have had any chance of maintaining a Nationalist foothold in the South of the country. Seeing Washington's reluctance to respond even to his demand for renewed mediation, on 21 January 1949, the Generalissimo announced his decision to withdraw. The Vice-President automatically became his successor and there was some slight hope that any further deterioration of the situation might be arrested. Yet it soon became clear that Li Tsung-jen lacked the necessary political experience and tended to overestimate his possibilities.

The Communists' eight-point peace terms were already known. They were uncompromising and admitted no bargaining with the Kuomintang. Yet the Acting President was convinced that the Communists would be prepared to negotiate a coalition on terms of equality with him or at least seriously to modify their original demands. His optimism was based on the conviction that with an army of still nearly two million men, with about half of China still under nominal Kuomintang control, and with the support of powerful allies, he commanded assets which would induce the Communists to seek a compromise. Soon he was to be disappointed.

The official retirement of Chiang Kai-shek did not prevent him from interfering in politics. Rather than improving the situation, his withdrawal, combined with his intrigues against the Acting President, merely helped to accentuate rivalries and dissensions within the Kuomintang. Whatever American inclination there was to provide further emergency aid to prop up the government, it was powerfully discouraged by the spectacle of continuing squabbles and accelerated demoralization within the Nationalist ranks.

Negotiations with Washington

In any case, rumours of stepped-up American aid were greeted with scepticism by all who had witnessed the Nationalist armies' performance. The American Chamber of Commerce in Tientsin sent its indignant protest. 'Americans in Tientsin who had the unhappy experience two months ago of witnessing the capture of Tientsin by Communist armies equipped almost entirely with American arms and other military equipment handed over practically without fighting by Nationalist armies . . .' said the message transmitted by the US Consul-General, '. . . feel the only result of further US aid to a Government which has proved so ineffective that most of our previous aid has passed to the Communists will be to further strengthen the Communists. . . .' Moreover, time was short. The Communist armies were massing along the Yangtze and no one knew when they would try to resume their advance.

Still continuing his attempts to obtain sufficiently spectacular promises from Washington to deter the Communists from crossing the Yangtze, Li Tsung-jen also sent a delegation to Peking trying to obtain the modification of the peace terms. In the meantime, the conflict of authority between Li and the Generalissimo and the resulting manœuvrings did nothing to change the evident lack of public support for the continuation of the civil war. The Communists could see that the Kuomintang was disintegrating and that the Nationalist armies had no will left to fight. Evidently, there was no reason for them to change their conditions.

In the meantime the Nationalist Government left Nanking and established its ministries in Canton. Significantly, the Russians were alone among the great powers to instruct their Ambassador to follow them to the South. The other diplomats were content to stay in Nanking and await the arrival of the Communist troops.

Although the Americans had repeatedly pointed out that there were enough arms and ammunition in the country to permit the organization of effective resistance, the Nationalist leaders continued to call for more spectacular forms of American intervention. To support their case they either spread rumours about faltering morale in the Communist ranks, or offered assurances concerning the massive resistance their armies would put up in case the Communists attempted to cross the Yangtze.

The Chinese Revolution

Finally, on 15 April 1949, the Nationalist Government was informed that it had five days to accept or to reject the draft peace agreement worked out with its delegation in Peking. In case of refusal or of no answer, it was said, the Communists would resume their advance.

On 20 April, just before the expiry of the ultimatum, the Nationalists requested a cease-fire so that further negotiations might be held.

The Communists cross the Yangtze

At midnight, on April 20 1949, the Communist forces crossed the Yangtze River at several strategic points. 'The ridiculously easy Communist crossing of the Yangtze,' the US Embassy informed Washington, 'was made possible by defections at key points, disagreements in the High Command, and the failure of the Air Force to give effective support.'

The Nationalist armies deployed for the defence of the river were hastily withdrawn. Behind them the three armies of Chen Yi, Lin Piao and Liu Po-chen spread out, covering the immense areas without encountering any serious resistance. Civilians and troops were sick of the war and the great cities fell one by one. Nanking, the symbol of Kuomintang rule, was occupied on 24 April. Hankow fell a month later. On 25 May, when the exhausted and inflation-torn city of Shanghai was entered, even Chiang's oldest allies, the bankers and the financiers, joined in the welcome to the disciplined columns marching in with their American equipment.

With inexhaustible vitality, the Communist armies continued their sweep, magisterially backed by propaganda, agrarian reform, and the ceaseless adaptation of political theory to the concrete problems encountered on their way. And while entire contingents, with their commanders and all their arms, continued to surrender, on 1 May the Generalissimo came out with a public statement expressing confidence in final victory though, he warned, the struggle might continue for three more years. While the Kuomintang intrigues continued, the tide of Communist victory was irresistibly running onward.

The final campaigns

During the summer the Communist armies, swollen by now by the Kuomintang legions incorporated after their surrender,

The Finale

overran Kiangsi, the cradle of the Red Army and of the Communists' first essay in government. Much of the North-west and Sinkiang too had come under their control. And by the autumn the Communist armies approached Canton whence, twenty-two years earlier, they had set out in the company of the Kuomintang to bring unity to China.

The Communists claimed that within a year they had destroyed or had obtained the surrender of over five million Kuomintang troops. The Americans maintained that not a single battle was lost for lack of arms, ammunition or other modern equipment. Meanwhile, Chiang Kai-shek, heading the Communists' list of war criminals, left the continent and, together with some remnants of his troops, took refuge on the island of Formosa. And with their departure, for the first time in a century China had a central government wielding effective power over the entire area of the country.

If in Russia the Communists were victorious eight months after the fall of the monarchy, in China it took thirty-seven years. During that long and painful search for a new certitude to replace the discredited old order, the combined forces of overpopulation and of explosive ideas did not cease to provoke extremism and violence. To control them China had to assimilate western organization and western technology. Yet looking back over that tragic period and remembering how cruelly humiliated the Chinese felt themselves to have been by the West, it may seem inevitable that they had to achieve their westernization in the form of an anti-western protest.

That, in a sense, was what Mao Tse-tung announced to the world from Peking when, on 1 October 1949, standing on the balcony of the Gate of Heavenly Peace, he read out the proclamation of the People's Republic of China. *The People's Republic*

Mao Tse-tung, who had adapted Marxist theory to the traditional Chinese method of peasant revolution, became the new Republic's first Chairman. Among the six Vice-Chairmen were Chu Teh, the architect of military victory, and the widow of Sun Yat-sen, the founder of the Kuomintang.

Of the twelve men who in 1921 founded the Chinese Communist Party in Shanghai, two only survived to be on that day on the balcony of the Gate of Heavenly Peace. Below them the enormous square was black with joyful crowds. They were celebrating the end of the Chinese Revolution; the one that was to remould the way of living of greater masses than any revolution in the long history of mankind.

Index

Index